THE
NEW ENGLAND
KITCHEN

· THE ·
NEW ENGLAND KITCHEN

FRESH TAKES ON SEASONAL RECIPES

**JEREMY SEWALL &
ERIN BYERS MURRAY**

PHOTOGRAPHY BY
MICHAEL HARLAN TURKELL

RIZZOLI
NEW YORK

New York · Paris · London · Milan

CONTENTS

PREFACE

My relationship with the shores of New England began as a young child when I would visit the exuberant summer towns of Cape Cod. Both of my parents were from Massachusetts, and family remained there as we made a life in the D.C. area. I have always identified with the region—I am a Red Sox fan, after all—and having recently moved to Boston I have gotten another view of the personality of New England life, in no small part due to Jeremy Sewall's cooking.

Jeremy is fluent in the ingredients, history, culture, and pride of New England like few other chefs. His lineage here gives him a perspective on the foods of this region that is at once contemporary and seasoned with the wisdom of previous generations. To eat Jeremy's food is to experience contentment. Every dish is an invitation to participate in the history that defines the spirit of New England.

The narratives and recipes in this book are a candid journey through the booms and busts of the region. The warm months are just a slice of the year-round life in these vibrant and historic communities. The vivid and still-abundant autumn leads to winter's dormancy; Jeremy refers to the land here in winter as "draped in a melancholy mood"—and indeed it is, save for the soulful and satisfying cooking that he shares with us in these pages.

Having spent time early in his career immersed in California cuisine at the Lark Creek Inn, Jeremy evokes all of the best aspects of the fresh food revolution. In all of his restaurants and here in this book he applies this perspective to the ingredients of his region to create meals that are accessible and easily prepared. He treats every ingredient as if it tells a story, as though each recipe represents an inheritance, which for Jeremy it does.

In *The New England Kitchen*, Jeremy gives us reason for hope. As a champion for his home "surf and turf," he works to support the communities that have long sustained the people and the rich culinary experience that have become national treasures.

What Jeremy shares with us is not only a study of a celebrated past, but also a statement on the delicious present and future of this dynamic region. Like the waves rolling onto the sandy beaches of Cape Cod, Jeremy's food invites you to take the plunge and dive into the flavors of a place for which we all should give thanks.

—BARTON SEAVER
DIRECTOR, HEALTHY AND SUSTAINABLE FOOD PROGRAM
CENTER FOR HEALTH AND THE GLOBAL ENVIRONMENT
HARVARD SCHOOL OF PUBLIC HEALTH

FOREWORD

I can trace the journey of this cookbook to the first time I dined at Jeremy's Brookline restaurant, Lineage, soon after it opened in 2006. That was the night I first experienced his butterscotch pudding. It was rich and smooth, but had a depth I couldn't pinpoint. It was better than any I'd ever tasted. I asked him about it after the meal and he gave me a small grin. "It's made with real Scotch," he said. That was the beginning of my love affair with Jeremy's food.

At the time, I lived close enough to the restaurant that it had become a regular stop, especially for special occasions. There's a wood-burning oven that sits at the center of the space, right behind the bar. To lounge in front of that oven on a frigid winter night in Boston is to experience something magical. My husband, Dave, and I would sit at the bar, inhaling the intoxicating aroma of roasted chicken, and feel like we'd completely escaped from the city. It was our go-to spot for both casual dinners and celebratory toasts.

And then my life took a turn. I'd been a lifestyle editor for a website and decided to take a hiatus from the media to work on an oyster farm in Duxbury, Massachusetts. Island Creek Oysters was well-known locally for its outstanding oysters; somehow, I convinced them to let me be a farmhand to get a feel for their world. A little later, I learned that Jeremy had been one of the first chefs to visit the farm, and that knowledge only deepened my appreciation for his commitment to local food. I spent eighteen months working on the farm and eventually turned the experience into a book, *Shucked: Life on a New England Oyster Farm*. Jeremy played a recurring character throughout, especially toward the end as I watched him and the farm's founder, Skip Bennett, partner to open the Island Creek Oyster Bar in October 2010.

Somewhere along the way (likely over a beer and a few oysters), Jeremy and I started talking about a cookbook. It was Jeremy's menu at Lineage that guided our decision to focus on New England cooking. Between his New England ancestry and our shared excitement for the change we were witnessing in the region's culinary landscape, it was a natural fit.

What we want to get across is that we've entered a new era in New England cooking. For too long, this region has endured a reputation for having a sturdy, traditional cuisine that offered little in the way of innovation or finesse. But we'd like you to forget the tired old association of baked beans, Yankee pot roasts, and lobster boils. Those iconic dishes no longer accurately re-

flect what is happening at the tables of so many New Englanders. A new generation of chefs, farmers, artisanal food producers, market owners, and fishermen are transforming the food landscape—while bringing us full circle and back to our roots. It's time for us to celebrate the wonderful ingredients that are available now. Our mission is to elevate the image of New England cuisine and celebrate a region that's strongly tied to its local bounty.

Jeremy is cooking as a contemporary New Englander—one who remains devoted to his roots but also is innovating constantly. Even though his cuisine may come across as refined and elegant at his restaurants, he loves a casual meal, especially when cooked outdoors and eaten by the water. For this cookbook, he's combined the best of both worlds. There are low-key, easygoing dishes like Classic Fried Clams (page 81) along with more challenging, expert options like Lobster-Stuffed Ravioli (page 46; my mom, Dottie Byers, a gracious recipe tester, can attest to its complexity). No matter where you start, you'll find delicious results. A few of my favorite take-aways are Jeremy's tips and techniques: Citrus as a seasoning is almost always your friend; perfectly pillowy gnocchi is possible to accomplish at home (the trick is drying the potato in the oven); and, most important, when it comes to working with ingredients, let Mother Nature be your guide.

It's been an absolute honor and pleasure to work on *The New England Kitchen*. I hope you get as much enjoyment out of it as I have.

—ERIN BYERS MURRAY
FOOD WRITER AND AUTHOR OF SHUCKED: LIFE ON A NEW ENGLAND OYSTER FARM

INTRODUCTION

There is no question that my heart belongs to the Northeast. It's the region that has defined my cooking since I first learned to crack a lobster. Both of my parents were born and raised in southern Maine, which means I spent almost every summer and holiday I can remember along the coastline there—it's the first place I go when I have any free time.

Like many chefs, my passion in the kitchen started at home. A number of the men on my father's side of the family are lobstermen in Maine. And it's no coincidence that many of the women on that side are versatile cooks. My parents, proud, industrious Mainers themselves, kept those sensibilities even while we lived in the Midwest. Most of our meals were homemade, and we had a garden in the summer that produced vegetables for canning and jarring that we could enjoy throughout the winter. Our meat was purchased from the local butcher and sweet corn came from a farmstand. Every summer, a trip home to Maine wouldn't be complete without filling up a cooler with lobsters and maybe some flounder or cod fillets to pack in the car with us. Some of my favorite memories take me back to family cookouts at my aunt and uncle's house on the York River on the southern coast of Maine. My aunt and grandmother would put piles of lobster tails and claws out, on two large picnic tables, alongside bowls of melted butter, salads of garden cucumbers and lettuce, blueberry pound cake, and the occasional hot dog for the less adventurous kids who refused to touch the lobster bits. And there it is: The roots of my love for simple, fresh food—food that's found to this day in backyards all over New England—can be traced back to those summer picnics. Those fundamentals will stay with me forever.

My family connection to New England runs deep. My ancestors came from Coventry, England, in the early 1500s; Henry Sewall was the first. He must have liked what he saw when he landed in Newburyport, Massachusetts, because he went back to England, picked up his family, and then returned to New England. Arguably the most famous of my ancestors was his son Samuel Sewall, who is known for his part in the Salem witch trials but accomplished much more than that. Over the years, members of the Sewall clan fought in wars, built bridges, farmed, and fished; one of us even became a chef. You could call us a pretty typical New England family.

Growing up, I always knew of Samuel but didn't have much interest in hearing the entire story. That changed when my wife,

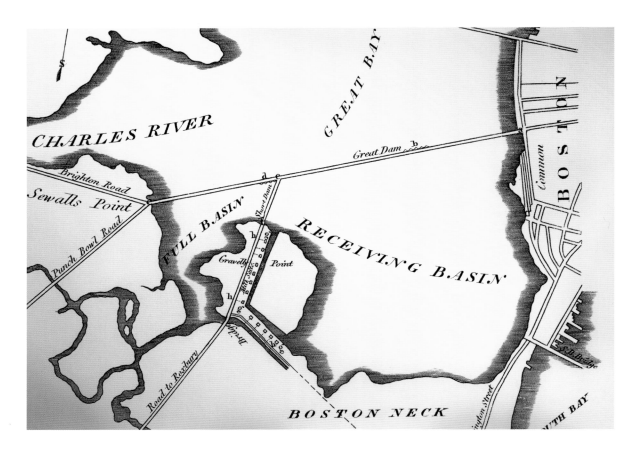

Lisa, and I were in the process of opening our first restaurant, Lineage, in Brookline, Massachusetts. After we picked out the property, I noticed a sign across the street that read "Sewall Avenue"; nearby sat the Samuel Sewall Inn. That led me to do a bit of research, which is when I learned that most of what is now Brookline was once owned by Samuel Sewall. His property stretched into what is now Boston and Kenmore Square—home to Fenway Park. The estate was called Brooklin and it was left to his son, Samuel, Jr., who turned it into the town of Brookline in the 1700s; Samuel, Jr., served as the town clerk. As far as I can tell, the original Samuel Sewall owned the land where two of my restaurants, Island Creek Oyster Bar and

Lineage, are now situated. I was also fascinated to learn about the Sacred Cod, a carved wooden figure that hangs in the state capitol building; the original cod that was given to the State Assembly of the Province of Massachusetts was thought to have been gifted by Samuel Sewall.

My career has taken me through a number of well-respected kitchens, from L'Espalier in Boston to the White Barn Inn in Kennebunk, Maine, and over to the the Lark Creek Inn in San Francisco's Bay Area. When I returned to Boston to open Lineage, it happened to be at a critical moment. During these years, New England has seen its own version of the culinary revolution that began in California in the '70s and '80s. When I started cooking

Today, New England is brimming with vibrant markets, some of which are open year-round. We have an amazing community of growers from the far reaches of Vermont, down to the coastline of Connecticut and Rhode Island.

here nearly twenty years ago, there were no farmers' markets, but we did have plenty of farmstands, especially in Maine. It was there where we got blueberries, corn, and other summer produce. Today, New England is brimming with vibrant markets, some of which are open year-round. We have an amazing community of growers, from the far reaches of Vermont down to the coastline of Connecticut and Rhode Island. New independent purveyors are constantly popping up, and every day we have the opportunity to taste something new. It's an exciting time to be a cook in New England.

But even as New England cuisine is in the midst of taking so many bold steps forward, I enjoy looking back at its history. Few areas of the country can boast so many iconic ingredients that are uniquely tied to this country's past and present. Atlantic cod helped shape our world and almost caused wars over its popularity and importance as a food source. How can you think about lobster and not think of Maine, where many in my own family have made a living since the 1930s? The first American apple orchard was planted in New England, in 1625. The source of maple syrup and cranberries, the birthplace of Thanksgiving . . . countless American food traditions essentially began in this area and have been imprinted on this country's culinary identity.

From its inception, American cuisine was all about the seasonal and regional because that was all the original inhabitants and early settlers had. No one was making salt cod and cured pork for the fun of it; it was necessary for survival during the harsh winter. And yet those ingredients are still seen daily on menus across the country—and even rise to the popularity level of "trends" now and then. Just like so many chefs across the country, I love reading old cookbooks, finding a classic dish, and re-creating it in a modern way to make it my own. More and more, I notice that our past is coming full circle. Thanks to small farmers, local fishermen, aquaculturists, market owners, and artisanal purveyors, who are putting their delicious, supremely local products into our hands, we are getting back to a time when those connections weren't trendy but simply a way of life. I relish these new ideas and find inspiration in their connection to the past. It's the reason why I find now to be the perfect time to be a cook in New England—and for a cookbook that captures all that I love about this region and the food that defines it.

—JEREMY SEWALL
OWNER OF LINEAGE, ISLAND CREEK OYSTER BAR, AND ROW 34; CONSULTING CHEF OF EASTERN STANDARD KITCHEN & DRINKS

SPRING

SPRING is the most unpredictable season in New England. There are usually a few warm days in March or April but, truthfully, these are raw, harsh months around here. Cold days overlap temperate ones, the ground starts to thaw, but nothing happens overnight. Just when you think it's time to ditch the coat, it snows on Mother's Day. I never know what to expect in the spring. It's a constant game of anticipation and appreciation. The true marker, to me, is the Red Sox home opener. Even if you don't love baseball, you can feel the change in the air here in Boston.

Two of the restaurants, Island Creek Oyster Bar and Eastern Standard, sit in the heart of Kenmore Square, steps from Fenway Park, and anyone who works at either spot will tell you that the energy is palpable. But it's more than just baseball. The warmer weather brings people out of hiding, and the farms and sleepy coastal towns start to come back to life. Like every New England season, it's time to get ready for the next—we're always anticipating what's to come.

What I look forward to most are the days when the fish and shellfish start showing up in New England waters. First, it's the oysters, which, after lying dormant all winter, are starting to pump that cold, crisp water that makes them taste pristine. Next come the mackerel. My sons and I love going out to catch mackerel; it's become our spring tradition. As soon as the season for groundfish opens, the restaurant kitchens start buzzing.

We'll see a few weeks of amazing spring cod and haddock from local day boats.

By that first warm day, we're craving ground-grown ingredients, but they trickle in slowly, one by one. The farmers' markets won't open until the end of the season, but I know my farmers are starting to get busy again. As they seed the ground and prep for the season, we rely on some of the wild options out there. We start with foraged ramps and wild mushrooms. That segues into early spring greens and herbs. It's a long process, but when we finally get to the point where we can put out basic salads, it's a celebration of truly simple pleasures. I love to surprise guests with a humble dish that also packs huge flavor: spring onions, green garlic, peas, and baby greens. Bright and vibrant and only available for a moment, the combination is the perfect introduction to the season.

SPRING

STARTERS

Smoked Salmon Crêpes WITH PICKLED RAMPS & CAVIAR	17
Raw Oysters WITH SPICY MIGNONETTE	21
Grilled Razor Clams WITH BACON & GREEN GARLIC	22
Steamed Mussels WITH PILSNER, GARLIC & FRESNO PEPPER	25
New England Cheese Board WITH SPICED NUTS & RHUBARB COMPOTE	26
Mushroom Ragout WITH FARM EGGS & TOAST	28
Spring Onion Soup WITH FENNEL & PARMESAN	31
English Pea Soup WITH CURRY CREAM	32
Baby Greens & Spring Vegetable Salad WITH DIJON VINAIGRETTE	35

MAINS

Day-Boat Cod WITH GREEN GARLIC PUREE	39
Poached Halibut WITH CRISP ARTICHOKE CHIPS	40
Baked Black Bass WITH MUSHROOM BROTH, SNAP PEAS & BUCKWHEAT PASTA	42
Pan-Roasted Shad Roe	45
Lobster-Stuffed Ravioli WITH ENGLISH PEAS & MORELS	46
Grilled Mackerel WITH LEMON & BABY FENNEL	49
Roasted Duck Breast WITH WILD RAMPS & CHERRIES	51
Whipped Ricotta Tortellini WITH MUSHROOMS, ASPARAGUS & FRIED GARLIC TOPS	52

SIDES

Fava Beans WITH SPRING ONIONS & NEW POTATOES	54
Roasted Apricots	56
Creamed Peas WITH GREEN GARLIC	57
Blanched Asparagus	57

SMOKED SALMON CRÊPES
WITH PICKLED RAMPS & CAVIAR

The season of ramps, the wild onions that grow throughout the Northeast, is a brief one that New Englanders treat like a celebration. To preserve the fleeting excitement, I quickly pickle ramps and serve them rolled up in a firmly textured crêpe with cured salmon. New Englanders have long been curing and smoking fish as a way to preserve their catch and survive long winters. Today, it's just as rewarding to take fresh salmon from raw to smoked. A couple of days are needed to cure the salmon, but it is well worth the effort.

Lay the crepes flat. Put a slice of smoked salmon on each (the salmon should cover about two thirds of the crêpe; make sure to do this on the part of the crêpe closest to you). Place 2 slices of avocado across the center and place the sliced ramps next to it. Spread a small amount of the crème fraîche at the top part of the crêpe, covering half the crêpe (this will help you create a seal). Fold the edge closest to you over the avocado and ramp and pull back slightly, tucking everything into the crêpe. Roll the crêpe into a tight cylinder shape, making sure the crêpe is even and firm. Trim off the ends. Slice each crêpe into five equal pieces. Spread the remaining crème fraîche on serving plates and place the sliced crêpes on top. Top each slice with a small spoonful of caviar and serve.

RECIPE CONTINUES

SERVES 8

---

8 Crêpes (recipe follows)

8 slices Smoked Salmon (recipe follows)

1 ripe avocado, cut in half, pit removed, thinly sliced

8 Pickled Ramps (recipe follows), thinly sliced on the bias

¼ cup crème fraîche

4 ounces salmon caviar

SMOKED SALMON

MAKES ENOUGH FOR
8 CRÊPES

1 cup kosher salt

3 tablespoons sugar

1 teaspoon freshly ground white pepper

1 teaspoon ground coriander

1 teaspoon ground fennel seeds

1 pound salmon fillet, skin on, bones removed

In a small bowl, mix together the salt, sugar, and spices. Sprinkle some of the salt mixture on a plate or tray, then place the salmon on top, skin side down, and cover with the remaining salt mixture on all sides. Refrigerate for 18 to 24 hours.

Remove the salmon from the refrigerator, rinse it and the plate under cold water, and pat both dry with paper towels. Put the salmon back on the plate and let sit uncovered in the refrigerator overnight.

Light a charcoal fire. Add hardwood chips or hardwood sawdust to the charcoal, then extinguish the flame but let the chips keep smoking. Set the salmon on a wire rack (a cookie cooling rack works great) and place the wire rack on top of the grill rack. Cover the grill. Let smoke for about 10 minutes with steady smoke, or a little longer if you prefer a smokier flavor. It is very important that you never let the internal temperature of the salmon get hotter than 100°F. If this happens, the fish will begin to cook, and that will change its texture. To help control the temperature, place a metal tray full of ice between the chips and the fish.

Remove the salmon from the grill. Place on a plate and let chill uncovered in the refrigerator for 1 hour before slicing. To slice, use a sharp knife and make very thin, horizontal cuts to produce pieces that are about the same thinness as the crêpes, about ⅛ inch thick.

PICKLED RAMPS

MAKES 12 RAMPS

12 ramps, roots trimmed

1 cup champagne vinegar

½ cup sugar

1 teaspoon fennel seeds

2 cardamom pods

1 teaspoon whole black peppercorns

1 tablespoon kosher salt

Place the ramps in a glass canning jar or other nonreactive heatproof jar root end down so that they are close together. In a medium saucepan, bring the remaining ingredients to a hard boil and pour the mixture over the ramps. Make sure the ramps are completely submerged. Let cool in the liquid for 24 hours before serving. The pickled ramps will keep, refrigerated, for up to 4 weeks.

CRÊPES

In a large bowl, whisk together the egg yolks, whole eggs, milk, and sugar until thoroughly combined. Whisk in the flour and salt; the batter will look lumpy. Pour through a fine-mesh sieve and refrigerate in an airtight container for 30 minutes or up to 2 days.

In a small nonstick sauté pan, melt the butter over medium heat. Pour ¼ cup of the batter into the hot pan, making sure it is evenly distributed. Let the crêpe cook for about 30 seconds, and using a thin spatula, flip the crêpe. Cook for 5 more seconds, then remove from the pan and place on a serving dish. Repeat with the remaining batter. Allow the crêpes to cool fully before assembling.

MAKES 12 CRÊPES
7 large egg yolks
5 large whole eggs
1 cup whole milk
1 tablespoon sugar
1 cup all-purpose flour
½ tablespoon salt
½ teaspoon unsalted butter

RAW OYSTERS
WITH SPICY MIGNONETTE

Oysters don't need much of anything—just lemon and a good shucking knife. But I do like to change things up on occasion with some great acid and a little spice. I developed this recipe for my friends at Island Creek Oysters who wanted something creative to offer when setting up raw bars. Add more Sriracha if you like more heat. The mignonette will last for a few days in the refrigerator but gets spicier the longer it sits.

Shuck the oysters (see page 232) and place them on a bed of crushed ice. Serve the oysters with the mignonette.

SERVES 6 TO 8

36 raw oysters

Spicy Mignonette (recipe follows)

SPICY MIGNONETTE

In a bowl, mix together all of the ingredients. Cover the bowl with plastic wrap and chill the mignonette in the refrigerator until ready to serve or for up to five days.

MAKES ½ CUP

2 large shallots, peeled and very finely minced

¼ cup white wine

¼ cup white wine vinegar

1 small jalapeño pepper, seeded and minced

1 teaspoon freshly ground black pepper

1 teaspoon Sriracha hot sauce

1 tablespoon chopped fresh flat-leaf parsley

GRILLED RAZOR CLAMS
WITH BACON & GREEN GARLIC

Razor clams are soft-shell clams that live in the mud flats along the New England coast. I love them for their unique texture and sweetness. I know a lot of fishermen and shellfish farmers who supplement their income by digging razor clams when the tide is right—sometimes as rarely as once a month, sometimes under the light of a full moon. But that's the beauty of these animals: They are wild and finicky and always a treat. Check with your local fish market or look for them online. A good purveyor will keep you informed about availability. And, just like you would with any shellfish, make sure they're alive when you buy them and that their shells are intact.

SERVES 4 TO 6

- 1 stalk green garlic
- 1 tablespoon canola oil
- 6 ounces Slab Bacon (page 242), cut into ¼-inch dice
- 20 medium-size razor clams, rinsed well
- 2 tablespoons roughly chopped flat-leaf parsley leaves
- Grated zest and juice of 1 lemon
- Kosher salt and freshly ground black pepper

Remove the outer layer of the green garlic and trim off the root end. Thinly slice until you reach the green part of the stem. Discard the greens, or save for another use.

In a medium sauté pan, heat the oil over medium-high heat. Add the bacon and render until it begins to crisp, 4 to 5 minutes. Remove from heat. Drain all but 3 tablespoons of fat from the pan. Place bacon back over heat and add the green garlic. Cook, stirring frequently, until the garlic begins to soften and becomes translucent, about 2 minutes. Let the bacon and garlic sit at room temperature while the clams are cooking.

Place the razor clams on a grill over high heat; cook until they begin to open, about 4 minutes. When the clams are cooked, place on a large serving platter. Warm and season the bacon and garlic with the parsley, lemon zest and juice, and salt and pepper. Spoon the bacon and garlic over the clams and serve.

STEAMED MUSSELS
WITH PILSNER, GARLIC & FRESNO PEPPER

Mussels are inexpensive compared to other shellfish, so it's easy to cook lots of them. They are grown mostly in Canada, but Maine has been producing some amazing mussels that are available throughout the year. The flavor is a little stronger than most shellfish, so they can stand up to steaming in beer. I prefer a lighter style of beer with some floral notes, such as a Pilsner, but try this recipe with whatever you're drinking that night.

In a large, heavy-bottom pan, melt the butter over medium-high heat; add the garlic, onion, and peppers. (Be sure to wear gloves or thoroughly wash your hands after handling the peppers.) Stirring constantly, cook until the garlic starts to color, about 1 minute, then add the mussels and beer.

Lower the heat to medium, cover, and let steam until the mussels open, about 6 minutes. Remove the pan from the heat and, with a slotted spoon, take the mussels out of the broth and place them in a large serving bowl. Bring the liquid back to a boil and stir in the cilantro and lemon juice; season with salt and white pepper. Pour the liquid over the mussels and serve with the toasted bread.

SERVES A GENEROUS PORTION TO 4

- ¼ cup (½ stick) unsalted butter
- 3 garlic cloves, thinly sliced
- 1 small red onion, thinly sliced
- 2 small fresno peppers, sliced into thin rounds, seeds discarded
- 3 pounds Maine mussels, washed, beards removed
- 1 (12-ounce) Pilsner beer
- ¼ cup fresh cilantro leaves
- 1 tablespoon freshly squeezed lemon juice
- Kosher salt and freshly ground white pepper
- 1 loaf Rustic Bread (page 230), sliced and toasted

NEW ENGLAND CHEESE BOARD
WITH SPICED NUTS & RHUBARB COMPOTE

A cheese expert, Molly Hopper Sandrof of Eastern Standard Kitchen & Drinks, offers her advice for putting together a cheese board: "New England's artisanal cheeses communicate a sense of place—they express the geography, terrain, and community that exist within this particular region. When putting together a cheese plate, we identify three important characteristics: milk type, texture, and strength of flavor. We usually recommend three cheeses so that you can taste the subtle flavors achieved from different milks. Select cheeses for texture, ranging from very soft to very hard. A well-designed cheese plate could include the spongy nature of a fresh goat; the luscious paste of a mold-ripened, cow's milk Brie; and the crumbly, mineral-driven texture of a blue cheese. Enjoy the salty brininess of a firm sheep's milk cheese before progressing to the earthy profile of a Vermont cow's milk cheese washed in heirloom apple cider."

For a few of our favorite New England cheeses, see New England Cheeses on page 246, and for our recommended New England cheesemongers, see Resources on page 244. Arrange your cheeses in order of flavor on a large serving platter. Serve with Spiced Nuts and Rhubarb Compote (recipes follow).

MAKES 2 CUPS

½ cup almonds

½ cup cashews

½ cup walnut pieces

½ cup salted peanuts

1 teaspoon chili powder

½ teaspoon ground cayenne

1 teaspoon dry mustard

1 teaspoon powdered sugar

2 teaspoons kosher salt

2 tablespoons melted unsalted butter

SPICED NUTS

Preheat the oven to 350°F.

In a small bowl, stir together all the ingredients. Spread on a half-sheet pan and bake until the nuts are lightly toasted, about 7 minutes, turning the nuts halfway through to ensure they toast evenly. Let cool, and store at room temperature in an airtight container for up to 5 days.

RHUBARB COMPOTE

In a saucepot, combine all the ingredients and simmer over low heat until the rhubarb is soft, about 40 minutes. Let cool, and store in an airtight container in the refrigerator for up to 2 weeks.

5 stalks rhubarb, cut into 1-inch pieces

1¾ cups dry white wine

1 cup sugar

1 teaspoon kosher salt

MUSHROOM RAGOUT
WITH FARM EGGS & TOAST

The appearance of morels is one sign that spring has arrived in New England. Morels are the perfect example of what a wild mushroom should taste like. There's a striking combination of both earthy and nutty flavors, and the honeycomb texture is unlike anything else. This simple dish can be made with most any mushroom but I love the combination of morels and peas especially. Be sure to use farm-raised eggs rather than ones that are mass-produced—you'll literally see the difference in the rich yellow yolk.

SERVES 4

4 slices Rustic Bread (page 230)

2 tablespoons extra-virgin olive oil

Kosher salt and freshly ground black pepper

3 tablespoons canola oil

8 ounces morel mushrooms, stems removed, washed, and cut in half

4 ounces shiitake mushrooms, stems removed, caps cut into quarters

1 large shallot, finely diced

2 garlic cloves, minced

1 tablespoon unsalted butter

2 cups Mushroom Stock (page 221)

½ cup shelled English peas, blanched

2 teaspoons sherry vinegar

4 large farm-raised eggs

Preheat the oven to 350°F.

Brush the bread with olive oil and season with salt and pepper. Toast in the oven for 5 to 7 minutes. Set aside at room temperature.

In a large sauté pan, heat the canola oil over medium-high heat. Add the morel and shiitake mushrooms and sauté until they begin to color lightly, 2 to 3 minutes. Lower the heat to medium; stir in the shallot, garlic, and butter. Cook until the butter is melted and the garlic is lightly toasted, another minute or two. Remove from the heat and carefully pour off any excess fat from the pan. Add the mushroom stock and return to the heat. Let simmer over medium heat, stirring occasionally, until reduced by almost half, about 8 minutes. Add the peas and season with the sherry vinegar, salt, and pepper. Keep warm.

Bring 1 quart salted water to a simmer and carefully break the eggs into the water. Poach for 2 minutes. The whites should be set, but the yolks will still be quite runny. While the eggs are poaching, place a piece of toast in each of four shallow bowls. Spoon the mushroom ragout over the top of the toast. With a slotted spoon, carefully spoon the eggs out of the water and place on top of the mushrooms. Serve warm.

SPRING ONION SOUP
WITH FENNEL & PARMESAN

I lighten up my cooking this time of year by incorporating lots of spring ingredients, but this luscious soup has a rich salty sweetness from the combination of fennel and Parmesan. The crisp prosciutto on top adds a layer of texture and brings together the flavors. Be careful when seasoning, since both the cheese and prosciutto increase the amount of salt in the finished soup.

Preheat the oven to 350°F.

Lay the prosciutto slices (if using) on a baking sheet lined with parchment paper, or a Silpat, and cover with another piece of parchment. Place a second baking pan, or an oven-safe dish, on top to keep the prosciutto flat. Bake for 4 to 6 minutes, until crisp. Let cool on the pan to room temperature until ready to use. Remove each slice carefully using a thin spatula.

Cut the root end off the spring onions and peel off the outer layer. Rinse the onions and cut into ¼-inch rounds up to the dark green part of the stem (save the greens for another use). Cut the fennel bulb in half and remove the core. Cut the fennel into 1-inch pieces.

In a large saucepan, heat the oil until lightly smoking. Stir in the fennel, spring onion, and potato; cook until the vegetables become translucent but don't color. Add the stock and Parmesan rind and bring to a simmer. Simmer gently for 5 minutes; add the cream, thyme, and bay leaf. Continue to simmer for 15 more minutes. Remove from the heat and let cool for 20 minutes.

Puree the soup in a blender until smooth. Pour through a fine-mesh sieve and return to a clean saucepan; just before serving, bring to a boil, then remove from the heat and whisk in all but 2 tablespoons of the grated cheese. Season with the lemon juice, salt, and pepper. Allow the soup to sit for 2 or 3 minutes, then whisk again to ensure that the cheese is fully melted and incorporated. Pour the soup into individual serving bowls and garnish with the prosciutto and the remaining Parmesan. Serve with slices of bread.

SERVES 6

- 6 slices prosciutto (optional)
- 2 bunches spring onions (about 6 onions)
- 1 fennel bulb, top removed
- 3 tablespoons canola oil
- 1 small Yukon gold potato, peeled and cut into 1-inch pieces
- 2 cups Vegetable Stock (page 220)
- 3 ounces Parmesan cheese, rind removed and reserved, cheese finely grated
- 1 cup heavy cream
- 2 sprigs fresh thyme
- 1 fresh bay leaf
- 1 tablespoon freshly squeezed lemon juice
- Kosher salt and freshly ground black pepper
- Crusty bread, such as Rustic Bread (page 230)

ENGLISH PEA SOUP
WITH CURRY CREAM

I love English peas when they're in season. I use as many as I can get my hands on—and when there's a really good harvest, this soup is my favorite way to take advantage. Be warned, though: It's a labor of love, since you have to shell a *lot* of peas to make a single batch. Before you buy peas, sample a few to be assured of their sweetness; peas can sometimes get a little starchy. Both parts of this soup can be prepared a day ahead; make sure both the peas and stock are cold when you puree them, to retain the bright green color.

SERVES 4

FOR THE SOUP

3 cups shelled English peas, blanched and shocked in cold water

2 cups Vegetable Stock (page 220), chilled

2 tablespoons canola oil

1 small Spanish onion, chopped

1 leek, white part only, washed and sliced

1 cup heavy cream

1 fresh bay leaf

2 sprigs fresh thyme

Kosher salt and freshly ground white pepper

FOR THE CURRY CREAM

½ cup crème fraîche

1 tablespoon ground yellow curry powder

1 teaspoon ground turmeric

1 teaspoon ground cardamom

Kosher salt

Make the soup: In a blender, puree the English peas with 1 cup of the stock until the puree is as smooth as possible. Add a little stock, if needed, to the blender to get a smooth consistency; it will be fairly thick. Refrigerate in an airtight container until ready to use.

In a large saucepan, heat the oil over medium heat; add the onion and leek. Sweat for 3 minutes, then add the remaining 1 cup stock, the cream, bay leaf, and thyme. Bring to a simmer and cook for 10 minutes. Remove from the heat and let cool to room temperature. Discard the bay leaf and thyme, then puree the soup base in a blender until smooth. Strain through a fine-mesh sieve and refrigerate in an airtight container for up to 2 days, until ready to serve.

Make the curry cream: Put the crème fraîche in a small bowl. In a small sauté pan, heat the curry powder, turmeric, and cardamom until fragrant but not burned, about 45 seconds. Remove from the heat and whisk into the crème fraîche. Season with salt.

To serve: In a saucepan, bring the cream soup base to a boil. Whisk in the pea puree and return to a boil. Lower the heat to a simmer and cook until the soup is warmed through, about 30 seconds. Season with salt and white pepper and pour into individual serving bowls. Top each serving with a dollop of curry cream.

Serve with Crab Beignets (page 111).

BABY GREENS & SPRING VEGETABLE SALAD
WITH DIJON VINAIGRETTE

At my restaurants we get excited about the first heads and cuttings of spring lettuces. They're usually pretty small but packed with flavor. I picked some of my favorite vegetables for this salad, but use whatever you like best. Choose the freshest greens available; they should be evenly colored, with a faint earthy fragrance. Baby greens should be very tender and delicate. The best way to store baby greens is loosely wrapped in a paper towel.

Make the Dijon vinaigrette: Remove the leaves from the thyme sprigs and put them in a blender, along with the shallot, garlic, mustard, lemon zest, 3 tablespoons cold water, and vinegar. Puree until smooth. Slowly add the two oils, making sure that the vinaigrette is emulsified (if it becomes too thick, add more cold water). The vinaigrette should have a smooth, creamy texture. Season with salt and pepper. Transfer the vinaigrette to an airtight container and refrigerate for up to 2 weeks.

Make the salad: Rinse off the radishes and cut into thin rounds. Cut the asparagus into thin strips on the bias, leaving the tips whole. Peel the baby carrots; then, using the peeler, shave the carrots into thin strips. Put the greens, peas, carrots, and asparagus in a large mixing bowl and dress with enough of the vinaigrette to just barely coat all of the lettuce leaves. Toss all of the ingredients gently to coat. Serve at once.

SERVES 4

FOR THE DIJON VINAIGRETTE

- 2 sprigs fresh thyme
- 1 small shallot, cut in half
- 1 small garlic clove
- 2 tablespoons Dijon mustard
- Grated zest of 1 lemon
- ¼ cup white wine vinegar
- ¼ cup extra-virgin olive oil
- ¾ cup canola oil
- Kosher salt and freshly ground black pepper

FOR THE SALAD

- 2 small breakfast radishes
- 5 stalks asparagus, blanched
- 3 baby carrots
- 3 cups mixed baby greens (such as red leaf, mizuna, and lollo rossa)
- ¼ cup shelled English peas, blanched

ISLAND CREEK
OYSTERS

Duxbury, Massachusetts
Skip Bennett

There was never a doubt in oyster farmer Skip Bennett's mind that he would make his living on the water. He did go to college and dutifully got his finance degree, but instead of considering a corporate job after graduation, he returned home to Duxbury, Massachusetts, and got busy digging clams.

It was the early '90s, and Skip had heard about shellfish farming on Cape Cod and out on the West Coast. Realizing that Duxbury Bay, with its vast ten-foot tides and mix of salt- and freshwater flow, was perfectly suited for farming, he started growing quahog clams. When his crop died suddenly from a common clam parasite, Skip switched to oysters. It turns out that farmed oysters thrive in Duxbury Bay. Within a few years, and with the help of a growing contingent of friends, he was harvesting thousands of oysters a week and selling them to Boston-area chefs.

Skip may have started out with little more than good instinct, but he quickly latched on to the idea that, like wine, oysters truly capture the taste of the place where they're grown. He calls that location-specific flavor profile "merroir," and it comes through clearly when you taste an Island Creek oyster. There's a distinct brininess as well as a crisp, almost sweetened finish. It's a direct result of both Duxbury's unique aquatic landscape and a massive amount of human energy. By harnessing the often volatile forces of nature that exist within the bay, Skip and the farmers at Island Creek can grow an oyster from seed to fully grown animal, all while allowing it to consistently and directly express the bay's sense of place.

The farm now produces around 5 million oysters a year, and serves as a distribution company, which sources oysters from New England and beyond. What's more, the team at Island Creek started its own nonprofit, the Island Creek Oysters Foundation, which works to provide aquaculture education to communities like Haiti and Zanzibar, Tanzania.

In 2010, I partnered with Island Creek and restaurateur Garrett Harker to open the Island Creek Oyster Bar in Boston's Kenmore Square, where the farm itself serves as the inspiration both in physical design and in philosophy. Our second venture, Row 34, opened in late 2013 with the goal of bringing the concept of a "working man's oyster bar" back into the American lexicon. It's taken a tremendous amount of hard work and ingenuity, but today Island Creek is considered one of the country's most beloved oyster farms.

DAY-BOAT COD
WITH GREEN GARLIC PUREE

Cod is the quintessential New England fish. There's a carved wooden "Sacred Cod" hanging in the House of Representatives in the Massachusetts State House. Some of this region's economies were built on the abundance of cod, and yet today the fish is a source of controversy—catch methods are under scrutiny. This is why I buy cod off of small day boats along the New England coast. This simple recipe allows for the cod's delicate flavor to emerge.

Preheat the oven to 300°F.

Zest the lemon and cut it into 4 wedges. Place the cod fillets on a baking sheet and top with the lemon zest, shallot, oil, salt, and white pepper.

Bake for 15 minutes. Pull the fish from the oven and squeeze the lemon wedges over the top. Place the fillets on individual plates and serve the green garlic puree on the side.

Serve with Crisp Fingerling Potatoes (page 224).

SERVES 4

1 lemon

4 (7-ounce) cod fillets

1 shallot, minced

2 tablespoons extra-virgin olive oil

Kosher salt and freshly ground white pepper

Green Garlic Puree (recipe follows)

GREEN GARLIC PUREE

Cut the garlic into thin rounds until you reach the green top. Slice the green tops into 1-inch pieces and separate from the white parts. In a medium saucepan, heat the oil over medium heat and sweat the white parts until they begin to color lightly, about 2 minutes. Add the cream and simmer for 10 minutes. Remove from heat and let cool to room temperature.

While the cream is cooking, bring a medium pot of salted water to a boil. Add the garlic greens to the boiling water and cook for 30 seconds. Drain and plunge the greens into an ice-water bath to stop the cooking. Drain the green tops well and use a paper towel to squeeze out as much liquid as you can. Put the tops in a blender with the garlic cream and puree until smooth. Season with salt and pepper.

MAKES 1 CUP

3 stalks green garlic

1 tablespoon canola oil

1 cup heavy cream

Kosher salt and freshly ground black pepper

POACHED HALIBUT
WITH CRISP ARTICHOKE CHIPS

Poaching fish might seem intimidating, but it can actually be more forgiving than roasting or sautéing. This recipe creates a moist and light piece of fish that pairs well with asparagus; the crunch of the artichokes completes the dish. Fry the artichokes a few hours ahead of the meal, since they'll stay crisp for a while.

SERVES 4

- 1 teaspoon plus ¼ cup unsalted butter
- 1 cup Vegetable Stock (page 220)
- ¼ cup white wine
- 1 fresh bay leaf
- 2 sprigs fresh rosemary
- 4 (7-ounce) halibut fillets
- 1 tablespoon freshly squeezed lemon juice
- 1 recipe Blanched Asparagus (page 57)
- 1 cup pea tendrils
- 2 teaspoons extra-virgin olive oil
- Kosher salt and freshly ground white pepper
- Artichoke Chips (page 227)

Preheat the oven to 300°F. Using the teaspoon of butter, grease a 9-inch square baking dish, or one that's just large enough to hold the halibut fillets in a single layer.

In a large saucepan, bring the stock, wine, bay leaf, and rosemary to a boil. While the stock is coming to a boil, place the halibut fillets in the prepared baking dish (they should fit snugly, but not overlap). When the stock has come just to a boil, remove from the heat and pour over the fillets; the liquid should come halfway up the fish.

Cover the dish with aluminum foil and place it in the oven; bake for 12 minutes. Use a cake tester or skewer to see if the fish is cooked. If you can pierce through it with little resistance, it's ready. Leave the oven on.

Remove the fish from the oven and pour about ½ cup of the poaching liquid into a saucepan; discard the bay leaf and rosemary. Bring the poaching liquid to a boil, then slowly whisk in the remaining ¼ cup butter. Remove from the heat and add half of the lemon juice.

Place the blanched asparagus on a baking sheet and bake for 3 minutes, until the asparagus is just warmed through. Remove the fish from the baking dish and place on a serving platter. Place a few whole asparagus on top of each piece of fish. Spoon the warm sauce over the fish and asparagus. In a small bowl, toss the pea tendrils with the remaining lemon juice and the olive oil; season with salt and white pepper. Top the fish with the pea tendrils and a few of the artichoke chips and serve.

BAKED BLACK BASS
WITH MUSHROOM BROTH, SNAP PEAS & BUCKWHEAT PASTA

Buying a whole fish is the best way to judge its quality. It should be shiny and look fresh; there should be no detectable odor or damage to the outside. This satisfying dish of earthy, fragrant flavors will become a favorite recipe. If you can't find black bass, try snapper or branzino.

MAKES TWO WHOLE FISH; SERVES 4

- 2 whole black sea bass, about 20 ounces each, cleaned and scaled
- 2 tablespoons extra-virgin olive oil
- Kosher salt and freshly ground white pepper
- 1 lemon, very thinly sliced
- 1 recipe (about 1 pound) Buckwheat Pasta Dough (page 229), cut into fettuccine
- 3 tablespoons canola oil
- 4 large shiitake mushrooms, stems removed, cut into thin strips
- 1 tablespoon minced fresh ginger
- 1 garlic clove, minced
- 4 scallions, green tops only, thinly sliced on the bias
- 1 small carrot, julienned
- 2 cups sugar snap peas, blanched and shocked

INGREDIENTS CONTINUE

Preheat the oven to 400°F.

Make sure that all of the scales have been removed from the fish. Rinse the outside and open cavity of the fish with cold water; pat dry. Using a very sharp knife, score the skin of each bass about four times on one side and place on a baking sheet. Rub the outside of the fish with the olive oil and season with salt and white pepper. Shingle the lemon slices on the top of the fish and place in the oven. Roast for 7 minutes, then lower the oven temperature to 300°F and roast for about 15 more minutes (the cooking time will vary depending on the size of the fish). Check doneness by piercing the fish with a skewer; the skewer should go through with minimal resistance.

While the fish is cooking, bring a large pot of salted water to a boil. Add the pasta and cook for 3 minutes, then drain and rinse with cold water. (The pasta will be only partially cooked at this stage.)

In a large sauté pan, heat the canola oil over medium-high heat. Add the mushrooms and cook until they begin to crisp lightly, 1 to 2 minutes. Stir in the ginger, garlic, and scallions and cook until they just begin to color, another minute. Add the carrot, peas, and stock; bring to a boil and let simmer for 3 minutes. Stir in the pasta, soy sauce, and vinegar and bring to a boil. As soon as the stock returns to a boil, remove from the heat and season with salt and white pepper.

Pour the broth and pasta into a large serving dish and sprinkle the cilantro and sesame oil (if using) over the top. Place the finished bass on a serving platter. To serve individual portions, spoon some broth and noodles into shallow bowls, then top with pieces of fish that have been sliced off the bone. (See How to Fillet a Round Fish, page 236.)

4 cups Mushroom Stock (page 221)

2 tablespoons soy sauce

1 tablespoon rice vinegar

1 tablespoon roughly chopped fresh cilantro

2 teaspoons sesame oil (optional)

PAN-ROASTED SHAD ROE

Shad is part of the herring family—typically, it's more prized for its roe than its meat because when the roe is full and ready the meat tends to be soft. When the shad are "running," they're coming from the ocean into freshwater rivers to spawn, much like salmon do. This is when they're harvested. The roe's striking and unusual taste stands up to big flavors like bacon, which is incorporated in this simple preparation.

Light a charcoal fire, or preheat a grill pan over medium-high heat.

Drizzle 1 teaspoon of the oil over the onion and season with salt and pepper. Place the onion rounds on the grill over medium-high heat, keeping the rounds intact. Shift the rounds by a quarter turn every minute for 4 minutes. Flip the onions and repeat. Set aside at room temperature.

In a large sauté pan, heat the remaining oil over medium heat. (Note that if the pan is too hot, the shad roe will split.) Season the outside of the roe with salt and pepper and add to the pan. Sear the roe for 4 to 5 minutes, until it begins to color. Carefully flip the roe and cook for 45 more seconds, then add the butter to the pan. Baste the roe with the butter and oil in the pan, then remove from the heat, leaving the roe in the pan. Let cool for 2 minutes.

To serve, arrange the bacon slices and onion rounds on the bottom of a serving dish and carefully place the roe on top. **Serve with Warm Potato Salad (page 224).**

SERVES 4

¼ cup canola oil

1 red onion, cut into ¼-inch-thick rounds

Kosher salt and freshly ground black pepper

1 pound shad roe (2 to 3 pieces)

2 tablespoons unsalted butter

4 slices Slab Bacon (page 242), cooked until crisp and kept warm

LOBSTER-STUFFED RAVIOLI

WITH ENGLISH PEAS & MORELS

For this fragrant dish, you can use different shapes or styles of pasta. I prefer small ravioli because they will cook through while keeping the lobster filling tender. If morels are not in season, substitute your favorite available mushroom.

SERVES 4

- 4 ounces wild morel mushrooms
- 2 tablespoons plus ½ cup kosher salt, plus more to taste
- 2 tablespoons canola oil
- 3 tablespoons unsalted butter
- Freshly ground white pepper
- 1 cup shelled English peas
- 2 (1¼-pound) lobsters, steamed, meat removed (see page 239)
- ¼ cup crème fraîche
- 2 tablespoons freshly squeezed lemon juice
- 1 tablespoon grated lemon zest
- 2 tablespoons chopped fresh flat-leaf parsley
- 1 recipe (about 1 pound) Plain Pasta Dough (page 227)
- 1 large egg, lightly beaten
- Flour for the ravioli
- ¼ cup pea tendrils

Trim the stems off the morels; if the morels are longer than 2 inches, cut them in half lengthwise. In a large container, combine ½ gallon room-temperature water and the 2 tablespoons salt; place the morels in the water and move them around to wash them. Quickly remove them and drain. (It's a good idea to do this more than once to make sure all the dirt and sand is removed from the morels.) Spread the morels out on a paper towel and let them air-dry for about 1 hour, or place them on a baking sheet lined with paper towels and dry them in the refrigerator overnight.

In a large sauté pan, heat the oil over medium-high heat. Add the morels to the pan without overcrowding them. Sauté the morels, stirring frequently, until they begin to color, about 1 minute. Add 1 tablespoon of the butter and season with salt and white pepper. Continue cooking until the butter begins to brown with the morels, 2 to 3 minutes. Remove the morels to a paper towel to drain. Set aside at room temperature.

In a large pot, bring 6 cups salted water to a boil. While the water is heating, fill a medium bowl with ice water, leaving enough room for the peas. When the water has come to a boil, pour all of the peas in at once and cook for 15 seconds, or until the peas are bright green and float to the top. Drain the peas and immediately plunge them into the ice water. Let cool, then drain and refrigerate in an airtight container until ready to use.

Cut the lobster meat into small pieces, about ¼ inch. In a small bowl, combine the lobster with the crème fraîche, 1 tablespoon of the lemon juice, the lemon zest, and the parsley;

RECIPE CONTINUES

place a second sheet of pasta on top. Starting at one end, use your fingers to push down all of the edges as you seal the ravioli and force out any air. Press a rolling pin over the edges of the mold to cut the pasta. [2] Remove and discard excess pasta pieces. Turn the mold over to gently release the ravioli. Repeat this process until you have 20 to 40 ravioli, depending on the size of your mold. Place the finished ravioli on a baking sheet and sprinkle with flour. Refrigerate, covered loosely with plastic wrap, until ready to cook.

When ready to serve, bring 2 gallons water and the ¼ cup salt to a boil.

In a large sauté pan, melt the remaining 2 tablespoons butter over medium heat. Add the morels and blanched peas and heat until just warmed through.

Add the ravioli to the boiling water. Let the water just barely return to a simmer and cook the ravioli for 3 minutes. Using a slotted spoon, remove the ravioli from the water and place them in the pan with the morels and peas. Add the remaining 1 tablespoon lemon juice and season with salt and white pepper. Carefully toss everything together and transfer to a large serving bowl. Top with the pea tendrils and serve.

RECIPE CONTINUED

season with salt and white pepper. Refrigerate in an airtight container until you're ready to fill the ravioli.

Cut the pasta dough into 2 pieces and roll through a pasta machine down to the second to lowest setting; the pasta should be just thin enough to see through. Make sure the pasta is a little wider than your ravioli mold and that it's cut the same length as the mold. Place a sheet of pasta on the ravioli mold and gently press the form over the dough to create a pocket for the filling. Remove the form and set aside. [1] Carefully fill each section of ravioli with the lobster—crème fraîche mixture so that it is full, but the ravioli can still be sealed with no filling coming out. (This amount will vary depending on the size of your mold.) Lightly brush the beaten egg around the edge of each filled section and

GRILLED MACKEREL
WITH LEMON & BABY FENNEL

Spring in New England is signaled by the arrival of Boston mackerel. The smallest of the mackerel family, it's a tasty fish kept whole. The smaller ones, called "tinkers," cook fast and easily. For a long time mackerel wasn't valued as an edible fish—even today, they're used more frequently as bait to hook larger fish or for lobster traps. But they're packed with flavor and "good" fatty acids, and they're also a cinch to prepare. Use this same cooking technique for bluefish or striper.

Light a charcoal fire, or preheat a grill pan over medium-high heat.

Pull a few of the fronds from the top of the fennel and reserve about 2 tablespoons. With a sharp knife or mandolin, shave the fennel bulbs down to the start of the cores (discard the cores). Refrigerate, covered with a damp paper towel, until ready to use.

Pat the mackerel dry and score the skin lightly three times on each side of the fish with a sharp knife. Whisk together the canola oil and 2 tablespoons of the lemon juice and rub a small amount on the outside of the mackerel; season both sides with salt and white pepper.

Place the mackerel on the hot grill, or grill pan, over medium-high heat, and cook for 2 minutes. Give each fish a quarter turn on the same side to create a grill-mark pattern. Flip the fish over and cook the same way on the other side.

While the fish is cooking, toss the fennel in a medium-size bowl with the remaining lemon juice and season with salt and white pepper. Let the fennel marinate for a few minutes. When the fish is done cooking, remove from the grill. Add the reserved fennel fronds, basil, frisée, and olive oil to the marinated fennel and toss well. Spread the fennel mixture on a platter and place the cooked mackerel on top. Serve family style.

SERVES 4

- 2 bulbs baby fennel with tops
- 8 Boston mackerel, about 4 ounces each, guts removed, rinsed well
- 1 tablespoon canola oil
- Juice of 2 lemons
- Kosher salt and freshly ground white pepper
- 12 small fresh basil leaves
- 1 head frisée, cored and cut into 1- to 2-inch pieces
- 3 tablespoons extra-virgin olive oil

ROASTED DUCK BREAST
WITH WILD RAMPS & CHERRIES

Ramps are wild onions that grow in wooded areas throughout the eastern United States in the spring. It's hard to miss them with their beautiful green tops. They can be found at specialty stores or while walking in the woods. They tend to be pungent, but roasting them tames the intensity a bit, making them a nice complement to duck—especially when you add the sweetness of cherries.

Preheat the oven to 375°F.

With a sharp knife, trim the fat around the edges of the duck breasts so that the fat is the same size and shape as the meat underneath. Score the fat lightly, cutting slits in one direction and then another to form a diamond pattern. (Be careful not to cut into the meat.)

In a large, heavy, oven-safe sauté pan, heat the canola oil over medium heat. Place the breasts in the pan fat side down and cook slowly so the fat renders off the breast and the skin begins to crisp to a golden-brown color, about 8 minutes. Transfer the sauté pan to the oven and roast for about 8 more minutes. The duck breasts will be medium rare. Remove from the oven and let rest for 10 minutes before slicing.

Lay the ramps on a large piece of aluminum foil and drizzle with the olive oil; season with salt and pepper. Fold the foil over to form a sealed pouch. Bake for 10 minutes.

In a medium saucepan, heat the chicken sauce over medium-low heat, then add the cherries. Increase the heat and bring to a low simmer (do not let it boil). Add the vinegar, then slowly stir in the butter. When the butter is melted, lower the heat and keep warm until ready to serve.

To serve, slice each duck breast into 6 pieces on the bias. Arrange the slices on a platter and spoon the cherry sauce on top. Lay warm ramps over the meat and serve.

Serve with Black Rice (page 194).

SERVES 4

- 4 duck breasts
- 2 tablespoons canola oil
- 12 wild ramps, washed and root ends trimmed
- 2 tablespoons extra-virgin olive oil
- Kosher salt and freshly ground black pepper
- ½ cup Chicken Sauce (page 181)
- 1 pound cherries, stemmed and pitted, cut in half
- 2 teaspoons sherry vinegar
- 1 tablespoon unsalted butter

WHIPPED RICOTTA TORTELLINI

WITH MUSHROOMS, ASPARAGUS & FRIED GARLIC TOPS

I love pairing green garlic and asparagus because, to my mind, it is a natural combination; they are two of the first bright flavors to arrive each spring. I use fresh pasta to tie these ingredients together. Look for a good ricotta, since it plays a starring role in this dish. And feel free to substitute oregano or rosemary for the basil.

SERVES 4 TO 6

1 cup ricotta

Kosher salt and freshly ground black pepper

6 large fresh basil leaves, cut into thin strips

1 recipe (about 1 pound) Plain Pasta Dough (page 227)

1 large egg, beaten

Flour for the pan

3 tablespoons canola oil

2 cups cremini mushrooms, washed and cut into quarters

2 tablespoons unsalted butter

1 recipe Blanched Asparagus (page 57)

1 tablespoon freshly squeezed lemon juice

Fried Garlic Tops (page 227)

Freshly grated Parmesan cheese

In a stand mixer fitted with the whisk attachment, beat the ricotta until creamy but still slightly lumpy, 2 to 3 minutes. Or, if whisking by hand, beat 4 to 5 minutes. Season with salt and pepper and fold in the basil. Refrigerate in an airtight container until ready to use.

Using a pasta machine, roll the dough out to the thinnest setting. Keep the sheets of dough lightly floured and covered. When all of the pasta has been rolled into sheets, use a 4-inch round cutter to cut circles out of the pasta dough.

To make the tortellini, lay the pasta rounds on a flat surface and place a little more than 1 teaspoon of the ricotta filling in the center of each circle. Lightly brush the beaten egg halfway around the edge of the pasta circle. Fold the edges of the circle together into a half-moon shape; starting at one end, press air out of the pasta with your finger. With the flat side closest to you, brush the left corner of the moon with the egg wash. Push the edge closest to you in slightly at the middle, then fold in the right corner, then the left corner to form the tortellini. Place finished tortellini on a floured pan and refrigerate until ready to cook.

Bring a large pot of salted water to a boil. While the water is coming to a boil, heat the oil in a large sauté pan over medium-high heat. Add the mushrooms to the sauté pan and

cook until they begin to color slightly, about 4 minutes, stirring occasionally so that they brown evenly. Remove from the heat and drain off any excess fat. Return to medium-high heat and add the butter; continue cooking until the butter melts. Stir in the asparagus.

Meanwhile, cook the tortellini in the boiling water for 1 minute; they should become slightly paler in appearance and float to the surface. Carefully scoop the pasta out of the water and place in the pan with the mushrooms and asparagus. Sauté for 30 seconds, moving the pan constantly. Remove from the heat; add lemon juice and season with salt and pepper. Toss everything together.

Spoon the pasta into 4 to 6 individual bowls; top with the fried garlic tops and Parmesan.

FAVA BEANS
WITH SPRING ONIONS & NEW POTATOES

Fava beans grow in a pod, like peas, but once you blanch the pods you need to peel each bean. I recommend that you blanch the shelled favas in boiling water for a few seconds, then let them cool in ice water before peeling so they stay nice and green. I'm also crazy about spring onions this time of year; their small, sweet bulbs and tender greens are easy to work with and they're mild compared to larger onions, which is why they play so well with the other flavors in this dish.

SERVES 4 TO 6

- 1½ cups small new potatoes, no more than 2 inches long
- 1 bay leaf
- 1 garlic clove
- 1 sprig fresh thyme
- Kosher salt
- 1 bunch spring onions (about 3 onions)
- 3 tablespoons unsalted butter
- 3 cups shelled fresh fava beans, blanched and peeled
- 2 tablespoons chopped fresh flat-leaf parsley leaves (optional)
- 2 teaspoons sherry vinegar
- Freshly ground black pepper

Wash the potatoes and put them in a stockpot with the bay leaf, garlic, and thyme. Cover with cold water and season well with salt. Bring the potatoes to a boil, then lower the heat and simmer until the potatoes are barely cooked through, 8 to 10 minutes. Remove the pot from the heat; let the potatoes cool in the water for about 10 minutes, then drain. When the potatoes are cool enough to handle, remove the skins by rubbing them with a paper towel, keeping the potatoes intact. Cut each in half lengthwise and set aside.

Trim the root ends off the onions. Thinly slice the onions on the bias until you get to the green stalk (save the greens for another use). In a large sauté pan, melt the butter over medium heat and add the onions. Cook until the onions just begin to soften, 1 to 2 minutes, then add the potatoes. Stir frequently and continue to cook for another 30 seconds, then toss in the fava beans. Cook until everything is warmed through; add the parsley (if using), vinegar, salt, and pepper. Toss well and serve at once.

ROASTED APRICOTS

I like most stone fruit by itself and raw. However, for this wonderful savory side dish, I pair apricots with rosemary—you can also serve roasted apricots with ice cream.

SERVES 4

¼ cup extra-virgin olive oil

2 sprigs fresh rosemary

6 ripe apricots

Kosher salt and freshly ground black pepper

Preheat the oven to 400°F.

In a small saucepan, heat the oil with the rosemary over medium-high heat until the rosemary just begins to sizzle, 1 to 2 minutes. Remove from the heat and let cool in the pan.

Split the apricots in half by cutting around the pit; remove the pit and lay each half face up on a baking sheet. Drizzle the rosemary oil over the apricots and season with salt and pepper. Bake for about 8 minutes, until soft but not mushy. Serve hot.

CREAMED PEAS
WITH GREEN GARLIC

Green garlic is mild and tasty; the green part is just as versatile as the white and purplish root end. English peas, which start to show up in markets just when I'm ready to shrug off winter, can easily be overpowered, but this combination with garlic and lemon brings out their bright green flavor.

In a large sauté pan over medium heat, melt the butter and cook until it begins to brown very lightly, about 2 minutes. Stir in the green garlic and cook until it begins to color, another 3 to 4 minutes. Pour in the cream and simmer until reduced by one third. (The time will vary depending on the size of the pan but should only take about 3 minutes.) Stir in the peas and simmer for another minute. Add the lemon zest and season with salt and pepper. Serve at once.

SERVES 4

2 tablespoons unsalted butter

2 small stalks green garlic, cut into thin rounds

1 cup heavy cream

2 cups shelled English peas, blanched

Grated zest of 1 lemon

Kosher salt and freshly ground white pepper

BLANCHED ASPARAGUS

Asparagus, like so many foods, is way, *way* better when you get it close to the source. For New England chefs, asparagus is a favorite because it's so versatile: You can steam it, grill it, or fry it.

Trim the woody ends off the asparagus and discard. Using a vegetable peeler or a sharp paring knife, gently peel the outer layer of the asparagus skin off the bottom third of the stems.

Bring 4 quarts water and the salt to a rapid boil. Meanwhile, prepare an ice-water bath. Drop the trimmed asparagus into the boiling water. Cook 15 to 25 seconds, until they are bright green. Drain and plunge the asparagus into the ice water. Serve immediately or refrigerate; the asparagus may be reheated in a warm oven or on the stovetop in a sauté pan.

SERVES 4

1 bunch asparagus

2 tablespoons kosher salt

SUMMER

I find it hard to describe the first truly warm New England summer day. We've made it through the winter's chills and the breezy air of spring. But the moment the first rays of the summer sun hit is pure magic.

For me, New England comes alive in the summer. Sleepy coastal towns become bustling hubs of activity overnight. Boats appear in the harbors. Ice-cream stands open instantaneously. The town roundabouts immediately bulge with too many vehicles.

Summer is the time when New England farmers and fishermen work the hardest and see the biggest rewards. As a chef, I get to experience that same cycle. The absolute best of summer ingredients—tomatoes, melons, corn, squash, striped bass, lobster, and clams—make their way into my kitchens. When you see a guy in a dusty hat walk through the back door at Island Creek Oyster Bar or Lineage, you know that summer has arrived. The local produce that's delivered might change daily depending on what's perfectly ripe. In June, that means strawberries, squash blossoms, and greens, and by August it's juicy tomatoes, fragrant basil, and peppers. It's important, both as a restaurateur and a home cook, to be flexible and have a fluid menu. And we always find a way to make the most of the ingredients that we've waited a whole year to see.

In the summertime, my motto is "Let Mother Nature do the work." The ingredients should shine—and while this isn't a new concept by any means, I personally feel it's the bravest thing we can do. Creating a simple salad or applying the most basic preparation to summer seafood makes a most memorable meal.

One of the important lessons I've learned as a New England chef is that geography should be your guide. Food always tastes better when eaten close to where it comes from: Enjoying a lobster roll at a picnic table in Maine while overlooking the ocean; popping back freshly harvested Cuttyhunk oysters on the farm's floating raw bar in Buzzards Bay; snacking on perfectly ripe heirloom tomatoes while still at the farmstand. These moments have given me a more complete appreciation for the food that's grown just outside my back door.

I like to take these memorable dining experiences and hand them over to guests by surprising them with simplicity. At some point during every summer, Lineage will offer a bowl of just-picked berries for dessert. It's not a dish I can do very often, but that's exactly what makes summertime so special. This is the season when we keep food pure and simple.

SUMMER

STARTERS

Hand-Dug Steamers WITH BAY LEAF & THYME	61
Herb & Pepper–Cured Salmon WITH MARINATED RADISHES & DILL	62
Fluke Crudo in Tomato Water WITH SEA SALT & CHIVES	65
Chilled New England Shellfish Platter	66
Farmers' Market Gazpacho	68
Broccoli Soup WITH CHEDDAR TOAST	71
Sweet Corn, Bacon & Crab Chowder	72
Garden Tomato & Goat Cheese Salad WITH BASIL	74
Grilled Peach & Fennel Salad	77
Tempura Squash Blossoms WITH WARM HEIRLOOM TOMATOES	78
Classic Fried Clams	81

MAINS

Roasted Bluefish WITH SWEET & SOUR PEPPERS	84
Wild Striped Bass WITH PARSLEY CREAM	87
Lobster BLT	88
Hand-Cut Fettuccine WITH LOBSTER KNUCKLES, GRILLED CORN & SWISS CHARD	91
Grilled Chicken	92

SIDES

Summer Squash & Tomatoes IN OLIVE OIL	93
Roasted Baby Beets WITH TOASTED RUSTIC BREAD	94
Ratatouille	97

HAND-DUG STEAMERS

WITH BAY LEAF & THYME

I was horrified the first time I watched my dad eat steamers. During a family trip to Maine we stopped at a roadside clam shack near Sebago Lake. I couldn't understand what he liked about such an odd-looking food. I've since come to appreciate these tender gems. This great communal dish, which showcases the flavors of the sea, is enhanced with fresh herbs. It can be shared at the picnic table to start a meal—preferably on the shore: Steamers always taste better near the water's edge and when freshly dug.

In a small saucepan over low heat, melt the butter with the thyme. Transfer about ¼ cup of the butter to a large saucepan set over medium heat; bring to a simmer. Add the garlic and shallots and sauté until they become translucent, about 2 minutes. Pour in the wine and bring to a boil. Add the clams, stock, bay leaves, and peppercorns. Cover tightly and steam until the clams have opened, about 5 minutes. With a slotted spoon, transfer the clams to a large bowl, leaving the liquid in the pan. Ladle about 1¼ cups of the cooking liquid from the top of the pan into a small serving bowl, making sure not to stir the liquid because any sand from the clams will settle to the bottom of the saucepan. Warm the remaining butter and place in a small bowl next to the bowl of cooking liquid.

To eat the steamers, remove the meat from the shell, peeling off the black covering from the "neck" of the clam. Rinse the meat in the cooking liquid to remove any sand, then dip into the melted butter.

(See image on page 59).

SERVES 4
1 cup (2 sticks) unsalted butter
6 sprigs fresh thyme
2 garlic cloves, minced
2 large shallots, minced
1 cup white wine
40 to 50 soft-shell clams, rinsed thoroughly
1 cup Vegetable Stock (page 220)
3 large fresh bay leaves
3 whole black peppercorns

HERB & PEPPER–CURED SALMON

WITH MARINATED RADISHES & DILL

Cured salmon pairs well with the subtle flavors of fresh radishes and dill. Keep an eye out for watermelon radishes, which are a lovely and flavorful alternative to the more common red variety.

SERVES 6 TO 8

- ½ cup kosher salt, plus more to taste
- ¼ cup sugar
- 1 tablespoon cracked black pepper, plus more to taste
- 1 tablespoon chopped fresh rosemary
- 1 tablespoon chopped fresh tarragon
- 1 tablespoon chopped fresh flat-leaf parsley
- Grated zest and juice of 1 orange
- 1 (2-pound) salmon fillet, skin on
- 8 red or breakfast radishes, very thinly sliced
- ¼ cup thinly sliced red onion
- 1 cucumber, peeled and thinly sliced
- 2 tablespoons freshly squeezed lemon juice
- 3 tablespoons extra-virgin olive oil
- 1 tablespoon roughly chopped fresh dill

In a small bowl, combine the ½ cup salt, sugar, 1 tablespoon pepper, rosemary, tarragon, parsley, and orange zest. On a piece of plastic wrap that is cut to about 12 inches square, sprinkle a little of the salt mixture, then place the salmon skin side down on top of the salt. Press the rest of the salt mixture into the salmon flesh. Fold the plastic wrap over the salmon to create a sealed package and place in a shallow pan in the refrigerator. Put something of equal size and weight (such as a small heavy pan) on top to gently press the salmon; let cure for 36 hours.

Remove the salmon from the plastic wrap and rinse off the salt mixture. (Covered in plastic wrap, the cured salmon will keep for 7 to 10 days in the refrigerator.) Place on a plate and refrigerate uncovered for 2 hours to dry it out.

While the salmon is drying, combine the radishes, onion, and cucumber in a medium bowl with the orange juice, lemon juice, and oil; season with salt and pepper and refrigerate for 45 minutes.

Drain most of the extra liquid from the radish mixture and spread the radishes on a large platter. Remove the skin from the salmon and very thinly slice the salmon at an angle. Carefully arrange the salmon slices on top of the radishes and sprinkle the dill over the top. Serve chilled.

FLUKE CRUDO IN TOMATO WATER
WITH SEA SALT & CHIVES

Fluke is one of my favorite fish to eat raw. Also called summer flounder, fluke is usually caught in the waters off of Rhode Island and Cape Cod. The flesh is firm and traditionally a beautiful ivory white. Fluke can be found at fish markets or online but keep in mind that it's best when in season. This recipe depends on fresh ingredients, so make sure the tomatoes are ripe and delicious. Note that you'll need to start this recipe at least a day in advance, as the tomato water needs to drain overnight.

Rinse the large tomatoes and remove the cores; chop into 2-inch pieces and put in a blender with the kosher salt and lime juice. Puree until very smooth. Line a fine-mesh sieve or colander with a coffee filter. Pour the tomato mixture through the coffee filter and let the tomato water drip through the filter overnight in the refrigerator. (This can be done 1 to 2 days in advance.) Pour the tomato water into an airtight container and keep refrigerated until ready to use.

Very thinly slice the fluke ; you should end up with 16 to 20 slices. Lay the slices out in a shallow container and pour half of the tomato water over the top. Let sit, uncovered, for 5 minutes in the refrigerator, then remove the fish from the liquid. To arrange, fold the slices in half on the serving plate (giving them a little bit of height). After arranging the slices, pour a little of the remaining tomato water over top. Sprinkle each piece of fluke with a pinch of sea salt. Place the cherry tomato quarters and radish slices randomly on the plate and garnish with the chives. Serve the crudo at once.

SERVES 4

- 2 large ripe red or yellow tomatoes
- 1 teaspoon kosher salt
- 3 tablespoons freshly squeezed lime juice
- 1 (8-ounce) fluke fillet, skin removed
- 1 teaspoon sea salt
- ¼ cup mixed cherry tomatoes, cut into quarters
- 1 radish, thinly sliced
- 1 teaspoon minced fresh chives

CHILLED NEW ENGLAND SHELLFISH PLATTER

Simplicity is the key when composing a shellfish platter, since all that's required are beautiful ingredients that are chilled and served with lemon and simple sauces. When assembling this dish, you'll put forth a large amount of effort up front but the results are impressive. I love to see the look on guests' faces when this abundance of shellfish arrives at the table.

SERVES 6

Crushed ice

12 raw oysters

12 raw littleneck clams

Ceviche (recipe follows)

3 lobsters, steamed, chilled, and cut in half (see page 239)

12 crab claws, steamed and chilled

1 lemon, cut into wedges

½ cup Spicy Mignonette (page 21)

½ cup Cocktail Sauce (page 223)

On a very large platter, or two smaller platters, place a few paper towels, followed by a 2-inch layer of crushed ice. Open and arrange the oysters and clams on the ice around the edges. Put the ceviche in a small bowl as a centerpiece in the ice. Place the lobsters and crab claws around the bowl and scatter the lemons over the top. Serve with the mignonette and cocktail sauce.

CEVICHE

In a large bowl, combine all of the ingredients; cover with plastic wrap and refrigerate for 2 to 3 hours. Serve chilled.

NOTE: If you don't have halibut, try fluke, bass, or scallops.

- 1 (1-pound) halibut fillet (see Note), cut into ¼-inch cubes
- ¼ cup freshly squeezed lime juice
- 2 tablespoons minced red onion
- 2 tablespoons minced cucumber
- 2 tablespoons chopped fresh cilantro
- 1 red radish, shaved into thin rounds
- 1 teaspoon minced jalapeño pepper
- Kosher salt and freshly ground white pepper

FARMERS' MARKET GAZPACHO

Never underestimate the impact of simple and seasonal produce. Using freshly picked vegetables—an assortment of heirloom tomatoes, peppers, and cucumbers—from the farmers' market makes a huge difference in this refreshing gazpacho. A jalapeño pepper will make the soup a bit spicier than the Fresno.

SERVES 6 TO 8

4 large red heirloom or beefsteak tomatoes

1 cucumber, peeled

1 red onion, peeled

1 red bell pepper, stemmed and seeded

2 garlic cloves, chopped

1 Fresno or jalapeño pepper, stemmed and seeded

½ cup freshly squeezed lime juice

¼ cup fresh cilantro leaves

Kosher salt and freshly ground black pepper

1 pint mixed cherry or grape tomatoes, cut in half or quarters

¼ cup extra-virgin olive oil

Rinse and core the tomatoes, then chop them into 1-inch pieces. Put the tomatoes and their juices in a large mixing bowl. Chop the cucumber, onion, and bell pepper into 1-inch pieces, dicing and reserving 2 tablespoons of each vegetable for garnish. Add the larger pieces to the bowl of tomatoes.

Add the garlic, Fresno pepper, lime juice, and all but 1 tablespoon of the cilantro to the other vegetables; mix well and season with salt and pepper. Cover the bowl with plastic wrap and refrigerate for 3 to 4 hours.

Transfer the mixture to a blender and puree. Strain the gazpacho through a fine-mesh sieve or a colander lined with cheesecloth (try to push through as much of the gazpacho as possible). Put the gazpacho in a large serving bowl, or individual bowls, and garnish with the diced vegetables, cherry tomatoes, and remaining cilantro. Drizzle the oil on top. Serve the gazpacho well chilled.

BROCCOLI SOUP
WITH CHEDDAR TOAST

There is something very comforting about a bowl of this rich broccoli soup—even during the height of summer, when broccoli thrives in the cooler regions of Maine. Cook the tops separately to give the soup a beautiful color and to intensify the flavor. Make sure to bring the soup to room temperature before adding the blanched broccoli to yield a bright green soup. Baguette slices topped with melted Vermont white cheddar pair beautifully with this soup.

Preheat the oven to 350°F.

Remove any large leaves from the broccoli and discard. Cut the bright green tops away from the stems. Peel the stems and cut into 1-inch pieces; cut the tops into similar-size pieces. In a large stockpot of boiling salted water, blanch the tops until tender, 1 to 2 minutes, then plunge into ice water to stop the cooking. (They should be cooked through but not soggy.) When cooled completely, remove from the ice water and refrigerate.

Heat the oil in a large saucepan over medium heat and add the onion, leek, potato, and broccoli stems. Sweat until the vegetables begin to soften (be careful not to let them brown), about 3 minutes, then add the stock and thyme. Bring to a boil, then lower the heat to medium-low and simmer for 10 minutes. Add the cream; season with salt and pepper. Continue to simmer for another 20 minutes, then remove from the heat and let cool to room temperature. Add the blanched broccoli to the soup and puree in a blender until very smooth. Strain through a fine-mesh sieve and return the soup to the saucepan.

Slowly bring the soup to a simmer and season with salt and pepper.

Lightly toast the baguette slices on a baking sheet in the oven for about 5 minutes. Sprinkle the toast with the cheese and return to the oven until the cheese melts, another 3 to 4 minutes. Serve the soup with the warm cheddar toast.

SERVES 6 TO 8

- 3 large heads broccoli with the stems
- 3 tablespoons canola oil
- 1 small Spanish onion, diced
- 1 leek, white parts only, washed and cut into ½-inch-thick rounds
- 1 Yukon gold potato, peeled and diced
- 3 cups Vegetable Stock (page 220)
- 2 sprigs fresh thyme
- 2 cups heavy cream
  Kosher salt and freshly ground black pepper
- 4 slices baguette, about 6 inches long and 1 inch thick
- ¼ cup grated white Vermont cheddar cheese

SWEET CORN, BACON & CRAB CHOWDER

Jonah crab is a local New England crab that until the 1990s was dismissed as a nuisance to lobstermen; the crabs would crawl into lobster traps and eat all the bait, and the discouraged lobstermen would have to dump the traps and start over. Now, Jonah crabs are considered a delicacy. I love pairing this sweet meat with smoky bacon and young corn—especially when the corn is fresh from a roadside stand. Corn is one of my favorite summer ingredients to cook with, and this soup is a great way to exploit its natural sweetness.

SERVES 6 TO 8

FOR THE SOUP BASE

6 ears corn, shucked, silk removed

3 cups Vegetable Stock (page 220)

2 cups heavy cream

2 sprigs fresh thyme

1 bay leaf

3 tablespoons canola oil

1 stalk celery, cut into 1-inch pieces

1 small Yukon gold potato, peeled and cut into 1-inch pieces

1 Spanish onion, peeled and cut into 1-inch pieces

1 small leek, white parts only, washed and sliced

Kosher salt and freshly ground black pepper

Make the soup base: Shave the corn kernels off the cobs and set aside. Put the cobs in a large stockpot and cover with the stock, cream, thyme, and bay leaf. Bring to a boil, then lower the heat and simmer for 20 minutes. Let cool. Pour through a fine-mesh sieve, saving the liquid but discarding the solids.

Heat the oil in a medium saucepan over medium-high heat and add the celery, potato, onion, leek, and half of the corn kernels. Reserve the remaining corn kernels for the soup. Sweat the vegetables for 3 minutes, stirring frequently, then add the stock from the corn cobs. Bring to a simmer and cook until the vegetables are cooked through, about 25 minutes. Season with salt and pepper. Let cool slightly, then, working in batches, puree in a blender until smooth. Strain through a fine-mesh sieve and refrigerate in an airtight container until ready to make the chowder.

Make the chowder: Put the diced potato in a saucepan filled with cold salted water and bring to a simmer; cook until the potatoes are tender but not falling apart, about 12 minutes. Drain and set aside.

In a large sauté pan, heat the oil over medium heat and add the bacon. Cook, stirring frequently, until the bacon starts to crisp, about 4 minutes. Carefully drain off most of the rendered fat, then add the celery, reserved corn kernels, and onion.

Sweat for 1 minute, then add the potato. Cook until just warmed through, then remove from the heat and fold in the crabmeat. Season with salt and pepper.

In a large stockpot, slowly reheat the soup base until hot, making sure that it doesn't stick to the bottom of the pot and burn. When it's heated through, add the lemon juice. Divide the soup among individual serving bowls and spoon the warm crab mixture into the center of each bowl. Garnish with the scallions and serve at once.

NOTE: If you don't have Jonah crabmeat, you can use lobster.

FOR THE CHOWDER

1 large Yukon gold potato, peeled and diced

2 tablespoons canola oil

1 cup diced Slab Bacon (page 242)

2 small stalks celery, thinly sliced on the bias

1 Spanish onion, diced

1 cup Jonah crabmeat (see Note), picked over and with any bits of shell removed

Kosher salt and freshly ground black pepper

1 tablespoon freshly squeezed lemon juice

2 scallions, green parts only, thinly sliced

GARDEN TOMATO & GOAT CHEESE SALAD
WITH BASIL

This simple tomato salad screams summer. Wait to make it until the tomatoes are at their ripest, toward the end of the season. I prefer simple red beefsteak or Early Girl tomatoes, but use whatever you have on hand. Slice the tomatoes at the last minute so they stay nice and juicy.

SERVES 6

1 cup goat cheese

¼ cup heavy cream

Kosher salt and freshly ground black pepper

3 large vine-ripe tomatoes

1 pint assorted cherry tomatoes

2 tablespoons extra-virgin olive oil

10 small fresh basil leaves

In a food processor, or with a bowl and a stiff whisk, combine the goat cheese and the cream until smooth. Season with salt and pepper. This mixture can be made in advance, covered, and refrigerated, but it should be brought to room temperature before using.

Spread a thin layer of the goat cheese mixture on a large serving platter. Using a very sharp knife, slice the tomatoes into equal rounds and shingle them on top. It is best to start on the outside of the platter and work toward the middle. Cut the cherry tomatoes in half and scatter them on top of the slices. Drizzle the oil over the salad, season with salt and pepper, and scatter the basil leaves on top. Serve at once.

GRILLED PEACH & FENNEL SALAD

I'm not usually a fan of cooking perfectly ripe peaches for anything but dessert. However, grilling them really changes the texture and flavor. Right off the grill, they are a nice complement to the raw, thinly sliced fennel used in this appetizer salad. Mizuna is a peppery green leaf that has the right amount of spice to balance out the sweetness of the fennel and peaches. You can usually find it at farmers' markets or specialty grocery stores, but arugula is a fine substitute.

Using a mandolin, or a very sharp knife, very thinly shave the onion and fennel. Put the shavings in a medium bowl and toss with the lemon zest and juice, salt, and pepper. Cover the bowl with plastic wrap and set aside to marinate at room temperature for 30 minutes.

Light a charcoal grill, or preheat a grill pan over medium-high heat. Cut each peach in half, top to bottom, and remove the pits. Brush the flat side of each half with oil and sprinkle with a little bit of salt. Place flat side down on the grill and cook until the peaches get a little charred, about 2 minutes. Rotate 45 degrees and cook for another 2 minutes. Let cool, then cut each half into six wedges.

Arrange the peach wedges on a large round plate, leaving space in the center of the plate for the fennel salad. Add the 3 tablespoons oil to the onion and fennel mixture and gently toss in the mizuna. Season with salt and pepper. Place the fennel salad in the center of the plate, sprinkle with feta, and serve.

SERVES 4 TO 6

- 1 small red onion
- 1 small bulb fennel, core and stalk removed
- Grated zest and juice of 1 lemon
- Kosher salt and freshly ground black pepper
- 2 large ripe peaches
- 3 tablespoons extra-virgin olive oil, plus more for grilling
- 2 cups lightly packed mizuna or arugula leaves
- ½ cup crumbled feta cheese

TEMPURA SQUASH BLOSSOMS

WITH WARM HEIRLOOM TOMATOES

This wonderful dish celebrates the tasty squash blossom. If you're lucky enough to find blossoms with the baby squash still attached, you should snatch them up and use the squash for another summer recipe. Squash blossoms are flowers, and they should be brightly colored and look fresh. They don't have a long shelf life, so cook them within a day of buying them.

SERVES 4

FOR THE TOMATOES

Kosher salt

4 heirloom tomatoes, different varieties

2 tablespoons extra-virgin olive oil

Sea salt and freshly ground black pepper

½ cup Basil-Arugula Pesto (recipe follows)

6 small fresh basil tops

FOR THE SQUASH BLOSSOMS

½ cup all-purpose flour

½ cup cornstarch

2 teaspoons baking powder

1 teaspoon baking soda

1 teaspoon kosher salt

½ cup soda water

4 to 6 ice cubes

12 squash blossoms

2 cups canola oil

Make the tomatoes: Bring a large pot of salted water to a boil and prepare an ice-water bath. Remove the core from each tomato and score the skin on the other end. Place in the pot of boiling water for 20 seconds, then remove and plunge into the ice water to stop the cooking. Peel the tomatoes. The skin should come off easily, but the texture of the tomato flesh should still be firm. Cut each tomato into 4 wedges; carefully remove the seeds and flesh from the inside so you are left with flat petals of tomato flesh. Cut into ½-inch pieces, gently coat with oil, and season with sea salt and pepper. (Save all the trimmings from the tomatoes for a sauce or soup.)

Make sure the tomatoes and pesto are at room temperature before frying the squash blossoms.

Make the squash blossoms: In a medium bowl, combine the flour, cornstarch, baking powder, baking soda, and salt; whisk in the soda water until there are no lumps. Add a few ice cubes to the batter to keep it cold. The batter should be thick enough to coat the blossoms, but the excess should run off easily.

Carefully open each blossom and, with tweezers, remove the stamen inside. Try not to tear the petals.

In a heavy-bottomed pan, heat the oil to 350°F on a deep-frying thermometer. Gently dip one blossom at a time into the

RECIPE CONTINUES

RECIPE CONTINUED

batter to coat. Holding on to one end, place half of the blossom in the oil; let it cook for 5 seconds before carefully releasing it into the oil completely. Repeat with the remaining blossoms. When the blossoms are crisp and very lightly browned, 45 seconds to 1 minute, remove from the oil and place on a paper towel-lined plate to drain. Season lightly with salt.

To serve: Spread a layer of pesto on a platter. Top the pesto with the heirloom tomatoes, leaving a little bit of the pesto exposed. Arrange the squash blossoms on top of the tomato, garnish with basil tops, and serve.

BASIL-ARUGULA PESTO

MAKES ABOUT 2 CUPS

2 cups lightly packed fresh basil leaves

1 cup lightly packed arugula leaves

1 cup lightly packed fresh flat-leaf parsley leaves

½ cup pine nuts, lightly toasted

½ cup finely grated Parmesan cheese

1½ cups extra-virgin olive oil

5 garlic cloves

Kosher salt and freshly ground black pepper

This simple pesto also goes well with blanched vegetables, and it can be served as a dip with good, crusty bread. I like my pesto smooth, so I use a blender, but you can make it in a food processor for a thicker consistency.

Put the basil, arugula, parsley, pine nuts, and cheese in a blender.

In a sauté pan over medium-high heat, heat the oil and whole garlic cloves for about 20 seconds, or until the oil temperature reaches 140°F.

Pour the oil and garlic over the ingredients in the blender and blend until smooth, 20 to 30 seconds. Immediately pour the pesto into a medium metal bowl set over an ice-water bath. Stir until cool; season with salt and pepper. Store the pesto in an airtight container in the refrigerator for up to 5 days.

VARIATIONS

The pesto can be made with either all basil or all arugula. Arugula pesto has a great bite to it that goes with almost any summer vegetable or is delicious as a dip with good bread. I heat the oil to cook the greens just a little. It gives the pesto a more floral flavor and a striking color. Basil pesto is a classic variation with a bright, well-rounded flavor.

CLASSIC FRIED CLAMS

Almost every coastal New England town has a clam shack, with the telltale smell of fryer grease in the air surrounding it. Everyone has his or her own personal favorite. For my family, a trip to Maine was not complete until we went to Bob's Clam Hut in Kittery—it's still one of my go-to spots when I want to order these crisp summertime treats. This dish is my version, which is inspired by these outings.

In a medium bowl, combine the clams, buttermilk, and Tabasco. Cover with plastic wrap and refrigerate for at least 1 hour or up to 1 day.

Preheat the oven to 200°F.

In a heavy-bottom pan or a counter-top fryer, heat the oil to 375°F on a deep-frying thermometer. While the oil is heating, combine the flour, mustard, turmeric, paprika, salt, and white pepper. Drain the clams and toss them in the seasoned flour; make sure they're well coated.

In two or more batches, place the clams in a fryer basket and lower them into the oil; fry until they are golden brown and crisp, 3 to 4 minutes. Remove the clams to a paper towel to drain off excess oil; season with salt. Put the first batch of fried clams on a baking sheet and place in the oven while cooking the rest.

Put the clams on a large platter in a single layer (don't stack them, or they'll become soggy). Serve with lemon wedges and tartar sauce.

SERVES 4

1 pound shucked fryer or Ipswich clams

½ cup buttermilk

1 tablespoon Tabasco sauce

4 cups canola oil

3 cups all-purpose flour

1½ tablespoons dry mustard

1½ teaspoons ground turmeric

1½ teaspoons paprika

1½ teaspoons kosher salt, plus more to taste

1½ teaspoons freshly ground white pepper

1 lemon, cut into wedges

Tartar Sauce (page 223)

WALKER'S
ROADSIDE STAND

Little Compton, Rhode Island
Coll Walker

Raising produce in New England requires an adaptable personality. Land is in short supply compared to in the vast heartland, and the seasons are extreme. Many farms in this area have been in the family for decades; newcomers are leasing whatever land is available. Coll Walker is part of the first group. He's a quirky guy with a wiry frame, cheek-length gray hair, and a fondness for Bob Dylan. His father purchased ten acres of farmland in the 1960s. After graduating from the University of Rhode Island, Coll joined the Peace Corps and went to work in Australia but came home three years later because his father had fallen ill. It was 1970 when Coll started running the farm. Since then he's expanded to about fifty acres by renting other plots nearby. It is a joy to walk through the fields with him and to be given a lesson on how corn is pollinated or to hear him expound on the virtues of the Sakonnet River, which flows right past his fields and fills the soil and produce with nutrients.

Coll opened one of the area's first farmstands, and now there are dozens run by other farmers. Customers who have been coming to his roadside stand for years find baskets brimming with red leaf, Boston or Bibb, and salad bowl lettuces, eggplant, pumpkins, strawberries, raspberries, zucchini, and beets. There's usually a wagon full of corn and melons in the high summer.

Not every year is a good year for Coll. An especially hot summer might bring brown or dying fields in August. But he plugs away. His son does more of the physical work these days, but Coll still runs the day-to-day operations at Walker's, where you can find him most summer days.

Coll doesn't sell to many chefs, and those who do buy from him, like me, swear by the consistency and flavor of his products. "I believe that if I present my produce beautifully, work hard, and offer people a fair price, the farm will thrive," he says. This philosophy continues to serve him well.

ROASTED BLUEFISH
WITH SWEET & SOUR PEPPERS

Bluefish is strong flavored—but not fishy tasting. It's probably more oily and richer than what many folks are used to, but this versatile fish stands up to bold summer flavors such as the peppers in this dish, which get a kick of tangy sweetness from the sherry vinegar. Most bluefish are line caught; they have a short shelf life, so cook them as soon as possible and handle them gently because the meat flakes easily.

SERVES 4

- 2 red bell peppers
- 2 yellow bell peppers
- 2 tablespoons sugar
- 2 tablespoons sherry vinegar
- ¼ cup Vegetable Stock (page 220)
- Kosher salt and freshly ground white pepper
- 1 teaspoon canola oil
- 4 (7-ounce) bluefish fillets, skin on
- 1 tablespoon Dijon mustard
- ½ cup panko bread crumbs
- 2 tablespoons sliced scallion greens

Preheat the oven to 400°F.

Cut the peppers in half, remove the seeds, and trim the inside white flesh. Cut into 1-inch strips, then cut the strips into diamond-shaped pieces by cutting at an angle every inch. In a medium-size sauté pan, combine the sugar and vinegar and bring to a boil over high heat. Add the peppers and cook for 30 seconds. Add the stock and simmer for 1 more minute; season with salt and white pepper. Remove from the heat and set aside at room temperature.

Rub the oil on a baking sheet and space the bluefish fillets evenly on the sheet. Rub the tops of the fillets with the mustard; season with salt and pepper. Top the fillets with a thin layer of bread crumbs. Bake for 8 minutes, or until cooked through; the bread crumbs should be lightly browned.

Warm the peppers on the stovetop. Divide the peppers among four individual serving bowls. Place the bluefish fillets over the peppers and garnish with the scallions. Serve at once.

WILD STRIPED BASS
WITH PARSLEY CREAM

Striped bass is a New England summertime staple. Most of this area's commercial catch comes out of Massachusetts. I usually serve this super-simple dish accompanied by my colorful Ratatouille, which makes for a beautiful presentation.

Preheat the oven to 350°F.

In a large oven-safe sauté pan, heat the oil over high heat. Season the fillets with salt and white pepper and place them skin side down in the pan. Press down lightly to make sure the fillets are flat in the pan. Sauté over high heat until the skin begins to crisp, about 3 minutes.

Place the pan in the oven and roast for 10 minutes. Remove the pan and carefully flip the fillets. Drizzle lemon juice over each fillet. To check that the fish is cooked through, carefully insert a skewer into the flesh; if there is light resistance, the fish is cooked.

To serve: Place each bass fillet over a spoonful of parsley cream and a small mound of ratatouille.

SERVES 4

- 3 tablespoons canola oil
- 4 (7-ounce) striped bass fillets, skin on
- Kosher salt and freshly ground white pepper
- Juice of 1 lemon
- ¼ cup Parsley Cream (recipe follows)
- 1 recipe Ratatouille (page 97)

PARSLEY CREAM

Preheat the oven to 375°F.

Put the shallot on a piece of foil and coat with the oil. Sprinkle with the salt, and tightly wrap the foil around the shallot. Roast for 10 to 15 minutes, depending on the size of the shallot. It should be tender if pierced with a skewer.

Put the parsley and roasted shallot in a blender. In a small saucepan, bring the cream to a boil. Turn on the blender and pour the hot cream into the blender. Puree until very smooth, then place in a small bowl that is set over ice to cool; stir frequently so that the puree cools down rapidly. Season with salt and white pepper. The parsley cream can be made in advance. Store in an airtight container in the refrigerator for up to 2 days.

MAKES ABOUT 1½ CUPS

- 1 large shallot, peeled
- 1 tablespoon olive oil
- ½ teaspoon kosher salt, or more to taste
- 1 cup flat-leaf parsley leaves
- 1¼ cups heavy cream
- Freshly ground white pepper

LOBSTER BLT

If you have any lobster meat left over after a lobster bake, enjoy my simple-to-prepare lobster BLT. It's a little fancier than a traditional lobster roll since it incorporates more summer classics—tomatoes and basil. I use red and yellow slicing tomatoes. If you like spice, add a little heat to the lobster meat with chile flakes.

MAKES 6 SANDWICHES

- 3 lobsters, steamed, meat removed (see page 239)
- 1 cup Herb Aïoli (page 222)
- 6 large fresh basil leaves
- 1 teaspoon freshly squeezed lemon juice
- Kosher salt and freshly ground white pepper
- ½ teaspoon chile flakes (optional)
- 18 slices Slab Bacon (page 242)
- 1 loaf Rustic Bread (page 230)
- ¼ cup unsalted butter, melted
- 2 red tomatoes
- 2 yellow tomatoes
- 1 head romaine lettuce, shredded

Cut the lobster meat into 1-inch pieces and toss with the aïoli. Rip the basil leaves into smaller pieces and add to the lobster meat. Season with the lemon juice, salt, white pepper, and chile flakes (if using), and refrigerate in an airtight container until ready to use. You can make the lobster salad up to 3 days in advance.

Preheat the oven to 350°F. Line a baking sheet with foil.

Lay the bacon in a single layer on the prepared baking sheet and bake until crisp, 10 to 12 minutes. Remove from the oven and drain the excess fat from the pan.

Cut the bread into ½-inch-thick slices and brush with the melted butter. Lightly toast on one side by placing in a medium sauté pan or on a grill over medium heat. Right before assembling the sandwiches, thinly slice the tomatoes (use only the center slices). Put half of the bread slices on a flat surface, toasted side down. Spoon the lobster salad onto the untoasted side, then add lettuce, a few tomato slices, and three strips of bacon to each. Top each with another piece of bread and serve.

HAND-CUT FETTUCCINE

WITH LOBSTER KNUCKLES, GRILLED CORN & SWISS CHARD

Lobster knuckles, at the "arm" of the lobster, where the claws connect to the body, are the most tender pieces of meat. If you're having a lobster feast, serve just the claws and tails and reserve the knuckles. And, if you don't have knuckles, you can make this dish with meat from the tails or claws.

Roll out the pasta dough thinly and cut into fettuccine. Spread out on a baking sheet, sprinkle with flour, and cover with a cloth; refrigerate until ready to use.

With a small knife, remove the entire stem from the Swiss chard by cutting a V shape into the leaf. Trim off the ends of the stems and thinly slice them crosswise. Tear the chard leaves into 2-inch pieces. Set aside.

Light a charcoal fire, or preheat a grill pan over high heat. Brush the corn with the oil and season with salt and pepper. Place the corn on the hot grill; cook until lightly charred, 2 to 3 minutes per side. Slice the corn kernels off the cobs.

Heat the remaining oil in a large sauté pan over medium-high heat and add the chard stems, garlic, and shallot; sauté until they begin to color lightly, about 2 minutes. Add the chard leaves and cook until just wilted. Add the grilled corn, stir, and cook for 1 to 2 minutes. Add the wine and bring to a boil; cook until the liquid in the pan is reduced to 2 tablespoons. Add the stock and return to a boil, then add the lobster meat. Cook for 30 seconds; stir in the butter. When it has melted, remove the pan from the heat.

Cook the pasta in a large stockpot full of boiling salted water and drain. Toss the pasta with the lobster, vegetables, and sauce in a large serving bowl. Season with salt, pepper, and lemon juice. Serve hot, family style.

SERVES 4 TO 6

- 1 recipe (about 1 pound) Plain Pasta Dough (page 227)
- Flour for the baking sheet
- 1 bunch red Swiss chard
- 4 ears sweet corn, shucked, silk removed
- 3 tablespoons canola oil
- Kosher salt and freshly ground black pepper
- 2 garlic cloves, minced
- 1 large shallot, thinly sliced
- ¼ cup white wine
- ¼ cup Vegetable Stock (page 220)
- 2 cups steamed lobster knuckle meat
- 3 tablespoons unsalted butter
- 2 tablespoons freshly squeezed lemon juice

GRILLED CHICKEN

For me, grilling and eating chicken outside is a summer joy. The simple marinade of this chicken dish intensifies once the meat has been charred on the grill. I prefer to buy whole chickens and break them down myself—if you are uncomfortable breaking one down, just buy it already cut into 8 pieces.

SERVES 6 TO 8

- 1 cup canola oil
- 2 scallions, roots trimmed off
- 2 garlic cloves
- 1 shallot
- Grated zest of 1 lemon
- 8 large fresh basil leaves
- 4 large fresh sage leaves
- ¼ cup fresh flat-leaf parsley leaves
- 2 whole chickens, about 3 pounds each
- Kosher salt and freshly ground black pepper

Put the oil, scallions, garlic, shallot, lemon zest, basil, sage, and parsley in a blender and puree until smooth.

Remove the wings and legs from the chicken, and separate the legs into thigh and drumstick pieces. Remove the backbone from the chicken and, with a sharp knife or scissors, cut the breast in two pieces, leaving the breast meat on the bones. You should have 8 pieces from each chicken. Put the chicken in a large bowl, pour the puree over it and toss to coat. Cover with plastic wrap, and put in the refrigerator to marinate for 4 to 6 hours.

Light a charcoal fire. Remove the chicken from the marinade, season with salt and pepper, and place on the hot grill. Sear the chicken until there is color on the outside, turning every couple of minutes to color all sides. The timing varies depending on the heat of the fire, but the outside should be crisp and slightly charred. Move the chicken to a higher rack or turn the grill to very low. Cover the grill and cook for 30 to 40 minutes, turning every 10 minutes. The smaller pieces will cook faster than the larger ones. To test for doneness, insert a thermometer into the thickest part of the meat; the internal temperature should be 165°F. Let rest for 10 minutes before serving. Serve hot.

Serve with Summer Squash and Tomatoes in Olive Oil (page 93).

SUMMER SQUASH & TOMATOES
IN OLIVE OIL

This simple squash dish will impress your family and friends. The vibrant colors of the vegetables look great when they're grilled and laid out on a serving platter. Make sure your grill is clean so that the vegetables do not stick to it. And consider adding an eggplant to the mix.

Light a charcoal fire, or preheat a grill pan over medium-high heat.

In a large sauté pan, heat 3 tablespoons of the oil over medium heat. Add the garlic and cook until it begins to color lightly, 1 to 2 minutes. Add the tomatoes and their juices and season with salt and pepper. (The mixture will become very loose and watery.) Cook, stirring frequently, until the tomatoes are softened and the sauce coats the back of a spoon, about 15 minutes. Lower the heat as the tomatoes cook down. Stir in the oregano (if using) and cook for 30 more seconds.

While the tomatoes are cooking, prepare the zucchini and squash: Cut the ends off and cut crosswise at an angle into ¼-inch-thick slices so the pieces are 3 to 4 inches long. Brush the zucchini, squash, and onion slices with the remaining 1 tablespoon oil and sprinkle with salt and pepper. Place on the hot grill and cook for 2 to 3 minutes on one side; flip the slices over and cook for 1 more minute. (The slices should have a little color from cooking but not be too soft or charred.) Remove from the grill.

Arrange the zucchini, squash, and onion on a large platter, spoon the tomato reduction in the center, and serve.

Serve with Grilled Chicken (page 92).

SERVES 6 TO 8

- 4 tablespoons extra-virgin olive oil
- 4 garlic cloves, smashed
- 6 red tomatoes, cored and cut into 1-inch pieces, plus all their juices
- Kosher salt and freshly ground black pepper
- About 20 fresh oregano leaves (optional)
- 2 zucchini
- 2 yellow squash
- 2 small red onions, peeled and cut into ¼-inch-thick rounds

ROASTED BABY BEETS
WITH TOASTED RUSTIC BREAD

Beets might make you think of fall, but summertime produces some amazing baby beets that come in vivid colors. I put these sweet, tender beets on a slice of crunchy toasted bread for a hearty open-faced sandwich. If you'd like to add another layer of flavor, spread a little Basil-Arugula Pesto over the toast.

SERVES 4

- 3 bunches baby beets with tops (about 12 beets)
- 2 tablespoons sherry vinegar
- 4 tablespoons extra-virgin olive oil
- Kosher salt and freshly ground black pepper
- 4 slices Rustic Bread (page 230), about 1 inch thick
- 2 tablespoons Basil-Arugula Pesto (page 80; optional)
- 1 tablespoon fresh oregano leaves

Preheat the oven to 350°F.

Trim the stems off the beets but leave about 1 inch of the top on each beet. Wash the beets and, in a shallow roasting pan, toss with the vinegar, 1 tablespoon of the oil, and the salt and pepper. Cover tightly with foil. Roast for about 50 minutes, until the beets are tender. (The best way to check doneness is to stab them with a toothpick, which should enter with light resistance.) Leave the oven on. Let the beets sit at room temperature until cool enough to handle, then carefully peel them by using a towel to rub off the skins. Cut the beets in half or quarters, then wrap them in a new piece of foil.

Brush the bread with 2 tablespoons of the oil and the pesto (if using). Place the bread slices on a baking sheet and toast in the oven until lightly browned, 5 to 7 minutes; at the same time, put the foil-wrapped beets in the oven to warm. Remove the bread and beets from the oven. Place the warm beets on top of the toasted bread and drizzle the remaining 1 tablespoon oil over them. Season with salt and pepper, garnish with the oregano, and serve.

RATATOUILLE

Ratatouille is the perfect excuse for a stop at the farmers' market. Select small squash and eggplant, since they'll have fewer seeds. Leave the skin on the eggplant, zucchini, and squash, as these vegetables' thin skins add great flavor and color. Make your cuts a little rustic for a hearty-looking dish; if you're serving the ratatouille with a delicate striped bass, dice the vegetables into uniform pieces for a more elegant presentation.

Heat the canola oil in a large sauté pan over medium heat until it begins to smoke lightly. Add the zucchini, squash, eggplant, bell pepper, and onion and sauté until the vegetables begin to color lightly, about 7 minutes. Add the garlic and tomato; sauté for another minute. Season with salt and black pepper. (If not serving the ratatouille immediately, drain off any excess oil and spread the ratatouille out on a baking sheet to cool. The ratatouille can be made 1 day in advance and stored in an airtight container in the refrigerator.) When ready to serve, warm the olive oil in a large sauté pan over medium heat and add the ratatouille to heat through. Transfer the ratatouille to a large serving bowl. Drizzle the vinegar on top and garnish with basil. Serve warm.

SERVES 4 TO 6

2 tablespoons canola oil

½ cup diced zucchini

½ cup diced yellow squash

¾ cup diced eggplant

½ cup diced red bell pepper

½ cup diced red onion

4 garlic cloves, chopped

½ cup diced tomato

Kosher salt and freshly ground black pepper to taste

1 tablespoon olive oil (if reheating)

2 tablespoons balsamic vinegar

3 large fresh basil leaves, torn

FALL

There is nothing quite like a New England fall. I love the way the air takes on the smoky aroma of burning wood stoves and fireplaces. And everyone talks about the rich palette of the fall foliage of New England—and I get it. Busloads of people come from around the country to enjoy the leaves. Honestly, it would be nice for us New Englanders if all of those folks took a few bags home with them. But the leaves are just a small part of why this season warms my heart.

So many great cooking opportunities present themselves in the fall. In our kitchen at Lineage, we look forward to its arrival. Despite having lusted for tomatoes and berries just a few short weeks back, our focus turns quickly to what this season brings: orchard apples, cider, big sweet squashes, Brussels sprouts, and cauliflower. The ingredients seem so indulgent after the clean, simple flavors of summer. Farmers' markets here now flourish in the fall as crafty farmers have found novel ways to make the most out of each season. There are heirloom squash varieties, dozens of types of potatoes, and all of the herbs and fixings for that perfect bowl of soup.

Venison was the first wild meat I ever ate during the fall hunting season, and it left a lasting impression on me. My dad had hit a deer with his Chevy one year and brought it home. Next thing I knew, I was cleaning the animal with the neighbor in the driveway. We had a freezer full of meat that lasted for months. I'm not sure I liked the texture at the time, but it seemed like a manly experience for a young boy.

As soon as the temperature drops and the winds pick up, we fire up the wood-burning oven at Lineage. The smell of oak-roasted chicken or fragrant mushrooms cooking beside an open fire is both comforting and palate pleasing. This is the moment when lobsters are at their peak and the oysters coming out of the colder water start to take on that unforgettable sweetness as they prepare to go dormant for the winter. Farm animals are fat and happy, ready to be harvested after feasting all summer, while the local fish season has hit its stride. There is nothing better than combining these rich flavors on the plate, pulling a chair up to the table, cracking open a frosty pint of cold, locally brewed beer, and savoring the most heartwarming of New England's dishes.

FALL

STARTERS

Crab Cakes WITH GRILLED SCALLIONS & PICKLED FRESNO PEPPERS OVER HUBBARD SQUASH PUREE	101
Fried Oysters WITH GREEN TOMATO RELISH	104
Bay Scallops WITH TASSO HAM & TRUFFLE OVER GREEN APPLE PUREE	106
Salt Cod Beignets WITH BLACK PEPPER AÏOLI	109
Goat Cheese Tart WITH POMEGRANATE & FRISÉE	112
Pear & Endive Salad WITH CRANBERRY VINAIGRETTE & TOASTED WALNUTS	114
Blue Cheese Croquettes	115
Lentil & Lobster Bisque WITH LEMON BROWN BUTTER	116
Sugar Pumpkin Salad WITH WHIPPED RICOTTA, TOASTED SEEDS & CURRY OIL	118

MAINS

Line-Caught Swordfish WITH CRISP BRUSSELS SPROUT LEAVES	122
Lobster Casserole	123
Seared Sea Scallops WITH CREAMY TURNIP PUREE & CRISP SHIITAKE MUSHROOMS	124
Spiced Skate Wing	127
Slow-Roasted Turkey WITH SIMPLE GRAVY	128
Grilled New York Strip Steak WITH MUSHROOMS IN RED WINE SAUCE	131
Maple-Brined Pork Rack WITH APPLES & LEEKS	134
Sage & Fennel–Stuffed Roasted Leg of Lamb	136
Roasted Venison Loin	138
Hand-Rolled Potato Gnocchi WITH ROASTED CHESTNUT PUREE & WILD MUSHROOMS	140

SIDES

Roasted Brussels Sprouts	145
Roasted Onions	146
Cauliflower WITH BROWN BUTTER & THYME	146
Vegetable Hash	147
Glazed Sweet Potatoes	148
Toasted Orzo WITH SPINACH & CHORIZO	149
Apple & Pomegranate Stuffing	150
Cranberry Chutney	151

CRAB CAKES
WITH GRILLED SCALLIONS & PICKLED FRESNO PEPPERS OVER HUBBARD SQUASH PUREE

This simple crab cake is a transitional fall dish. The Fresno pepper topping provides the perfect spicy accent to the crunchy crab cakes, and the earthy sweet squash puree adds a mellow touch to the flavors. Every coastal region of the United States has its favorite crab. Jonah crab isn't as well-known as blue crab or other varieties, but personally I think this medium-size crab makes a delicious crab cake. If you can't get fresh Jonah crab, buy precooked, prepackaged Jonah from a trusted source (see Resources, page 244).

In a large bowl, combine the crabmeat, bell pepper, onion, lemon juice and zest, mayonnaise, egg, cilantro, and Tabasco sauce. Add the bread crumbs a little at a time (the mixture should be moist but not wet), mixing until the batter can be balled up and still hold its shape. (There will likely be bread crumbs left over.) Weigh the mixture into 4-ounce balls and shape into cakes that are about 3 inches in diameter. Gently press each side of the cakes into the remaining bread crumbs to coat the tops and bottoms but not the edges. Refrigerate, covered with plastic wrap, until ready to cook.

In a medium saucepan, bring the vinegar, sugar, and tablespoon of salt to a boil and pour over the sliced Fresno peppers. (For spicier peppers, pickle them with their seeds. If you like less heat, clean out the seeds. Wash your hands thoroughly after handling the peppers.) Let sit until cool; drain off the excess liquid.

Light a charcoal fire, or preheat a grill pan or sauté pan over high heat. Brush a little oil on the outside of the scallions and sprinkle with salt and pepper. Place the scallions on the hot grill and cook, turning them often to get an even char on the outside. Remove the scallions from the grill and let cool; thinly slice them on the bias. In a medium bowl, toss the scallions with the pickled Fresno peppers.

RECIPE CONTINUES

MAKES 6 CRAB CAKES

- 1 pound fresh Maine crabmeat, drained and picked over, any bits of shell discarded
- ¼ cup minced red bell pepper
- ¼ cup minced red onion
- Juice and grated zest of 1 lemon
- 6 tablespoons Homemade Mayonnaise (page 222)
- 1 large egg
- 2 tablespoons chopped fresh cilantro
- 1 tablespoon Tabasco sauce
- 3 cups panko bread crumbs
- ½ cup champagne vinegar
- ½ cup sugar
- 1 tablespoon kosher salt, plus more to taste
- 4 Fresno peppers, cut into thin rounds

INGREDIENTS CONTINUE

¼ cup canola oil

6 scallions, ends trimmed off

Freshly ground black pepper

Hubbard Squash Puree (recipe follows), warm

Heat the remaining oil in a medium sauté pan over medium heat and add the crab cakes; brown slowly on each side, 3 to 4 minutes per side. Remove to a paper towel to drain.

To serve, place a dollop of the puree on each individual plate, place a crab cake on top, then top with the pickled peppers and scallions.

HUBBARD SQUASH PUREE

MAKES ABOUT 2 CUPS

This recipe can be made with most types of fall squash, such as acorn and butternut, without adjusting the cooking time.

In a medium saucepan, melt the butter until it begins to bubble. Add the squash and apple and cook until the mixture begins to color lightly, about 5 to 7 minutes. Add the cream and sage leaves; simmer for 10 minutes.

Transfer the mixture to a blender and puree until smooth; season with salt, pepper, and lemon juice. Refrigerate in an airtight container until ready to use. To reheat, put the mixture in a medium saucepan and slowly bring to a simmer over low heat.

3 tablespoons unsalted butter

1 cup peeled and diced Hubbard squash

¼ cup peeled and diced McIntosh apple

1½ cups heavy cream

2 fresh sage leaves

Kosher salt and freshly ground black pepper

1 teaspoon freshly squeezed lemon juice

FRIED OYSTERS
WITH GREEN TOMATO RELISH

If you have a garden in New England, you'll need a couple of handy green tomato recipes. Otherwise, you'll be kicking yourself once that first frost hits. I make relish from unripe tomatoes that would otherwise die on the vine. It is a perfect complement to briny oysters and other seafood. I double-bread the oysters to make them really crisp on the outside but creamy once you bite into them. Note that you can prepare all the components a day ahead.

SERVES 8

32 medium to large oysters, carefully shucked, bottom shells reserved (see page 232)

1 cup all-purpose flour

8 large eggs, whisked with 4 tablespoons water

6 cups panko bread crumbs

2 cups kosher salt, plus more to taste

3 cups canola oil

½ cup Smoked Paprika Aïoli (page 222)

Green Tomato Relish (recipe follows)

Wash the bottom shells of the oysters and scrape off any remaining oyster meat; set aside. Drain any liquid from the oysters.

Pour the flour into a medium bowl. Divide both the eggs and bread crumbs in half, placing each half in separate medium bowls. (Once half of the oysters are breaded, use the remaining egg and bread crumbs; this technique will cut down on cross-contamination.) Carefully roll each oyster in the flour so it is completely covered; shake off any excess. Dip the oysters into the eggs, then in the bread crumbs, making sure they are completely coated. Dip the oysters a second time into the eggs, and then coat with the bread crumbs. Cover the oysters with plastic wrap and refrigerate for up to 24 hours packed in some bread crumbs to absorb any moisture.

Just before frying the oysters, in a small bowl, mix the salt and ¼ cup water to create a thick paste and set aside. The paste will be shaped into mounds and used as a pedestal to hold the oyster shells for presentation.

In a wide, heavy-bottom pan, heat the oil over medium heat to about 350°F. Carefully fry the oysters, a few at a time, until golden brown, turning them halfway through as needed, about 45 seconds per oyster. Transfer the oysters to a paper towel–lined plate and sprinkle with salt.

On a large platter, place nickel-size dollops of the salt paste around the platter, placing a reserved shell on each dollop. Place one warm oyster in each shell and top with a small amount of aïoli and then a little relish. Serve immediately.

GREEN TOMATO RELISH

Finely chop the tomatoes, onion, and peppers. Place in a fine-mesh sieve (or a large colander lined with cheesecloth) and drain for 30 minutes, stirring every 10 minutes.

In a small saucepan, heat the remaining ingredients over medium heat until the sugar has dissolved. Transfer the tomato mixture to a heat-proof container and pour the pickling liquid over the mixture. Refrigerate in an airtight container for at least 2 hours or overnight. The relish will last, refrigerated, for up to 2 weeks.

MAKES ABOUT 4 CUPS

- 6 medium green tomatoes
- 1 large Spanish onion
- 2 red bell peppers
- 2 cups white wine vinegar
- ¼ cup kosher salt
- ¼ teaspoon ground cloves
- ½ teaspoon ground ginger
- 1 teaspoon celery seeds
- 1 (3-inch) cinnamon stick
- ½ cup sugar

BAY SCALLOPS
WITH TASSO HAM & TRUFFLE OVER GREEN APPLE PUREE

With its smoky notes of ham and the tart sweetness of green apples, this dish feels like a decadent celebration of fall. Nantucket bay-scallop season usually starts in November, but the temperature has to be just right: cold enough, but not so cold that the scallops freeze when they come out of the water. They're always harvested by hand by fishermen standing in waders in frigid, chest-deep waters, using long nets to scoop the scallops off the bottom. They're a splurge, which is why I often pair them with fresh truffles.

SERVES 4

- 2 tablespoons unsalted butter
- 8 ounces Nantucket bay scallops (20 to 25 scallops)
- Kosher salt and freshly ground black pepper
- 4 ounces Tasso Ham (recipe follows), finely diced
- 1 teaspoon freshly squeezed lemon juice
- Green Apple Puree (recipe follows)
- 2 tablespoons diced apple (reserved from the Green Apple Puree)
- Leaves from 2 sprigs fresh flat-leaf parsley
- 1 small black truffle, very thinly shaved

In a medium sauté pan, heat the butter over medium heat until it just starts to brown. Season the scallops with salt and pepper and add them to the pan; sauté, moving constantly for 20 seconds or until the outside of the scallops begin to brown. Stir in the ham and cook for 10 more seconds. Remove from the heat and add the lemon juice.

Drop and drag the puree across a serving platter and carefully spoon the scallops and ham onto the puree, leaving any excess fat in the pan. Garnish with diced apple, parsley, and shaved truffle.

TASSO HAM

Tasso ham is not that hard to make and, when done right, has the perfect balance of smoke and spice. It can be shaved thin and eaten as is but makes a great addition to dishes when diced and sautéed.

In a small bowl, combine the salt and all of the spices. Rub the pork with all but ¼ cup of the spice mixture. In a dish large enough to hold the pork in one layer, sprinkle 2 tablespoons of the spice mixture on the bottom and lay the pork on top; sprinkle the remaining 2 tablespoons of the spice mixture over the top. Cover the pork tightly with plastic wrap and refrigerate for 2 days. Flip the pork and cover again; refrigerate for 1 more day.

Preheat the oven to 300°F.

Light a very small charcoal fire in an outdoor grill, or turn on one burner of a gas grill.

Soak the wood chips in water for 20 minutes; drain well. Place the chips on the fire; when they start to smoke, add the pork to the grill and cover. Smoke for 15 to 20 minutes (if the chips catch on fire, spray with a little water; you want to avoid any flames) until the pork turns a smoky brown color. Turn the pork once during the smoking process.

Transfer to a roasting pan and roast in the oven until a meat thermometer inserted into the thickest part of the pork registers 165°F, 1 to 2 hours (the time will vary depending on the size and shape of the pork). Let the pork cool. Place in an airtight container and keep refrigerated for up to 8 days.

RECIPE CONTINUES

MAKES ABOUT 1 POUND

½ cup kosher salt

4 tablespoons freshly ground black pepper

3 tablespoons freshly ground white pepper

2 tablespoons paprika

2 tablespoons ground cayenne

1 teaspoon ground allspice

1 teaspoon ground cinnamon

1 teaspoon freshly grated nutmeg

½ teaspoon ground mace

3 pounds boneless pork butt or shoulder, cut into 2 uniform pieces

2 cups apple- or oakwood chips

RECIPE CONTINUED

GREEN APPLE PUREE

MAKES ABOUT 2 CUPS

2 Granny Smith apples, cored

1 cup white wine

1 small shallot, thinly sliced

Leaves of 2 sprigs fresh thyme

½ cup heavy cream

Cut the apples into 1-inch pieces, reserving one piece, and put them in a medium saucepan with the wine, shallot, and thyme; bring to a simmer and cook for 5 minutes. Add the cream and simmer for another 3 minutes. Transfer the mixture to a blender and puree until smooth. Serve warm. The puree can be made 1 day in advance. Store in an airtight container in the refrigerator, and before serving, reheat in a small saucepan over low heat.

Dice the reserved apple to use as a garnish for the scallops.

SALT COD BEIGNETS

WITH BLACK PEPPER AÏOLI

Traditionally, cod was preserved with salt so that it could be transported to Europe. Salting cod results in great textural and flavor changes to the fish, plus it's super simple to do. This recipe is easy to prepare when the ingredients are warm or at least room temperature before you begin. The beignet batter should be made just before you are ready to fry—if it sits around for too long or is refrigerated you won't get the same results.

Preheat the oven to 350°F.

Rinse the salt cod thoroughly. (If using store-bought salt cod, soak it in water overnight in the refrigerator.) In a medium saucepan, place the rinsed cod in the milk and bring to a boil. Remove from the heat and let sit at room temperature for about 15 minutes.

In a large pot, put the potatoes in cold, salted water and bring to a simmer; cook until tender but not mushy, about 15 minutes. Drain and place on a baking sheet.

Dry the potatoes in the oven for 5 minutes, then remove from the oven and put through a ricer. If you don't have a ricer, grate the potatoes on a box grater.

In a small sauté pan, heat the 2 tablespoons oil over medium heat and cook the onion until it is translucent (don't let it color), about 2 minutes. Remove from the heat and stir in the rosemary.

Remove the cod from the milk, breaking it apart with your hands. Place the pieces in a large mixing bowl. Stir in the potato, pâte à choux, and onions. This step may be done either with a stand mixer fitted with a paddle attachment, or your hands.

In a high-sided sauté pan or wide, shallow saucepan, heat 3 to 4 cups oil, enough to cover the beignets at least halfway, to 350°F. Using a 1-ounce ice-cream scoop, carefully place one level scoop of the pâte à choux mix in the oil. Repeat with 7 to 9 more scoops for the first batch. (If you add too many, the oil temperature will drop too rapidly.) Fry the beignets until they

RECIPE CONTINUES

MAKES ABOUT 38 BEIGNETS

- 1 pound Salt Cod (recipe follows; or use store-bought)
- 2 cups whole milk
- 2 pounds russet potatoes (about 4), peeled and cut into 2-inch pieces
- Kosher salt
- 2 tablespoons plus 3 to 4 cups canola oil
- 1 small Spanish onion, finely diced
- 1 tablespoon finely chopped fresh rosemary
- 1 cup Pâte à Choux (recipe follows), at room temperature
- 1 cup Black Pepper Aïoli (page 222)

are golden brown, flipping so that they cook evenly. The outside should be crisp; the inside should be firm but creamy. Carefully transfer them to a paper towel—lined plate to drain. Repeat with another batch until the batter is gone. Place the beignets in a serving dish and serve with aïoli on the side.

VARIATION
CRAB BEIGNETS

Replace the salt cod with 12 ounces fresh, picked-over Maine crabmeat. Wring out any excess moisture with a dry towel. Cook using the same method as above just before serving.

SALT COD

Bury the cod in the salt and refrigerate for 6 hours. (The cod can remain covered in salt for up to 24 hours but the longer it sits, the more intensely salty the fish becomes.) Thoroughly rinse the cod before using.

MAKES ABOUT 1 POUND

1 pound fresh cod fillet, no skin

1 cup kosher salt

PÂTE À CHOUX

In a medium saucepan, combine ½ cup water, the milk, and butter; bring to a rolling boil. Remove from the heat and add the flour, sugar, and salt all at once. Stir immediately with a wooden spoon, then put the saucepan back over the heat. Stir until the dough forms into a ball and leaves a film on the sides and bottom of the pan.

Put the hot dough mixture in the bowl of a stand mixer fitted with the paddle attachment (or place in a medium bowl and use a wooden spoon). Mix constantly until the dough is cool and no longer steaming.

When the dough is cool, add the eggs one at a time, mixing after each addition until fully incorporated. The final dough should be thick and glossy. Wrap the dough in plastic wrap and keep refrigerated for up to 2 days.

MAKES ABOUT 2½ CUPS

½ cup whole milk

7 tablespoons unsalted butter

1 cup all-purpose flour

¾ teaspoon sugar

½ teaspoon kosher salt

4 large eggs

GOAT CHEESE TART
WITH POMEGRANATE & FRISÉE

This delicious tart combines the classic fall flavors of pomegranate and apple. A simple Vermont goat cheese works well in the filling. Many dairy farmers in New England have turned to artisanal cheesemaking and dairy production, and Vermont in particular is known for producing some of the best cheese and dairy in the region.

MAKES 1 (12-INCH) TART

FOR THE DOUGH

1½ cups all-purpose flour

¼ teaspoon kosher salt

9 tablespoons unsalted butter, diced

2 large egg yolks

¼ cup heavy cream

FOR THE FILLING

8 ounces soft Vermont goat cheese

5 ounces heavy cream

2 large whole eggs

1 teaspoon fresh thyme leaves

Kosher salt and freshly ground black pepper

TO SERVE

1 head frisée lettuce, root end removed, leaves washed

Seeds from 1 pomegranate

2 tablespoons Dijon Vinaigrette (page 35)

Kosher salt and freshly ground black pepper

12 Fuji apple slices

Make the dough: In the bowl of a stand mixer fitted with the paddle attachment (or with a wooden spoon), combine the flour and salt. Gradually add the butter until the mixture becomes crumbly and the butter is reduced to pea-size pieces.

In a small bowl, combine the egg yolks and cream and pour into the flour mixture. Paddle, or stir, until the dough comes together in a ball.

Remove the dough from the bowl, wrap tightly with plastic wrap, and refrigerate for at least 1 hour before rolling out.

Position a rack in the center of the oven and preheat to 350°F.

On a lightly floured surface, roll out the dough until it is an even ⅛ inch thick. Place the rolled-out dough in a 12-inch tart pan, trimming off any excess. Make sure to press the dough firmly against the sides of the pan. Prick the dough with a fork and place the dough-lined pan in the freezer for about 20 minutes, until the dough is firm.

Bake the tart crust for about 8 minutes. The dough should be partially baked.

Make the filling: In the bowl of a stand mixer fitted with the whisk attachment (or in a mixing bowl), whisk the goat cheese with all the other ingredients until smooth. The mixture should have the texture of lightly whipped cream. Pour into the par-baked tart shell and smooth the top so it is level.

Bake for 25 minutes; a little color on top is fine.

Toss the frisée and pomegranate seeds together with the vinaigrette, then season with salt and pepper. Arrange the salad and apple slices on top of the warm tart. Cut the tart into wedges and serve.

PEAR & ENDIVE SALAD
WITH CRANBERRY VINAIGRETTE & TOASTED WALNUTS

This simple salad celebrates fall's bounty. It depends on good-quality pears, such as Bosc or Bartlett, that are perfectly ripe. Endive, frisée, and cranberries can be naturally bitter, but the sweetness of the pear coupled with the orange and spicy cayenne balances the dish.

SERVES 4 TO 6

- ¼ cup walnut pieces, or almonds
- 4 tablespoons simple syrup (equal parts water and sugar, dissolved)
- 1 teaspoon ground cayenne
- 1 teaspoon kosher salt, plus more to taste
- ½ cup fresh cranberries
- 1 small sprig fresh rosemary
- 2 tablespoons extra-virgin olive oil
- 2 heads Belgian endive, root end removed, leaves separated and washed
- 2 large ripe Bosc or Bartlett pears
- 1 cup frisée lettuce leaves, washed
- Grated zest of 2 oranges

Preheat the oven to 350°F. Line a baking sheet with parchment paper and coat with nonstick cooking spray.

Toss the nuts with 2 tablespoons of the simple syrup, the cayenne, and 1 teaspoon salt. Drain off excess liquid and place the nuts on the prepared baking sheet. Bake for 10 minutes. Let cool.

Put the cranberries, rosemary, and remaining 2 tablespoons simple syrup in a small saucepan and bring to a boil. Simmer for about 3 minutes; remove from the heat. Reserve 2 tablespoons of the cooked cranberries in a small bowl. Discard the rosemary sprig, transfer the remaining cranberry mixture to a blender, and puree until smooth. Add the oil in a slow, steady stream. Let the cranberry vinaigrette cool to room temperature.

Take the largest of the endive leaves and lay them on a serving platter. Core the pears and thinly slice them. In a large bowl, toss the pear slices with the frisée, orange zest, smaller endive leaves, and cooled cranberry vinaigrette; add a pinch of salt. Place the mixed salad on top of the endive, leaving the points of the large leaves uncovered and sticking out a little. Top the salad with the reserved cranberries and nuts and serve immediately.

BLUE CHEESE CROQUETTES

For my blue cheese croquettes, I use the robustly flavored Great Hill blue cheese, from Marion, Massachusetts. The beauty of this cheesemaking operation is that they make only one kind of cheese, and it is produced to perfection. I like to eat it in chunks, but this is one of the few blue cheeses that also works well when cooked. The croquettes make beautiful hors d'oeuvres, or you can pair them with bold flavors like a good steak such as my Grilled New York Strip Steak (page 131).

Preheat the oven to 350°F.

In a large stockpot, cover the potatoes with cold water and add the salt. Simmer until cooked through but not mushy, about 10 minutes.

Drain and place on a baking sheet. Dry in the oven for 5 minutes.

Put the potatoes through a food mill or grate on a box grater into a large mixing bowl. Add the cheese, pâte à choux, and sage leaves to the potatoes; mix the ingredients thoroughly until everything is incorporated (a few visible pieces of cheese is fine). At this point the mixture should be left at room temperature until ready to cook.

In a heavy-bottom pan, heat the oil to 300°F. Using two small spoons (or a small 1-ounce ice-cream scoop), shape the cheese mixture into quenelles. Carefully drop each ball into the oil and fry until golden brown, 5 to 6 minutes. Don't add more than 5 or 6 pieces to the oil at a time, or the oil will cool down too quickly. Remove the croquettes to a paper towel-lined plate to drain. Season with salt and serve immediately.

(See image on page 132).

MAKES ABOUT 2 DOZEN

- 2 russet potatoes, peeled and cut into 1-inch pieces
- 1 tablespoon kosher salt, plus more to taste
- 3 tablespoons crumbled blue cheese, preferably Great Hill
- ¼ cup Pâte à Choux (page 111)
- 3 large fresh sage leaves, chopped
- 2 cups canola oil

LENTIL & LOBSTER BISQUE

WITH LEMON BROWN BUTTER

Bisque is traditionally thickened with rice or lobster shells, but lentils also make great purees and so it wasn't a stretch to use them in this hearty soup. The lentils thicken the stock and so not many lobster shells are needed. Plus, they add an earthy flavor that marries well with the shellfish.

SERVES 6

¼ cup canola oil

1 (1½ pound) lobster, steamed (see page 239), meat removed, shell reserved, 1 cup of the meat cut into ½-inch pieces (reserve the remaining for another use)

1 small carrot, peeled and sliced

1 small Spanish onion, peeled and diced

1 stalk celery, sliced

2 tablespoons tomato paste

½ cup plus ¼ cup green lentils

½ cup brandy

5 cups Lobster Stock (page 219)

1 small muslin bag containing 3 to 4 sprigs fresh thyme, 1 bay leaf, and 4 or 5 whole black peppercorns

INGREDIENTS CONTINUE

In an 8-quart stockpot, heat the oil over medium-high heat. Cut the shells of the lobster body and tail into 4 equal pieces and add to the oil. Stir frequently until they start to color; add the carrot, onion, and celery and continue to cook until the vegetables begin to soften, about 5 minutes. Drain off any excess oil and stir in the tomato paste. Cook for 30 seconds, stirring frequently to make sure it doesn't burn. Stir in ½ cup lentils and brandy. Let the brandy evaporate (this should only take about 30 seconds), then add 4 cups of the stock and the bag of aromatics. Bring to a boil, then lower the heat and simmer for 30 minutes. Add the cream and continue to simmer for another 10 minutes.

Remove the mixture from the heat and let stand at room temperature for 15 minutes. Remove the bag. Puree the mixture in batches, including the lobster shell pieces, in a blender until smooth. Make sure to divide the shell pieces equally among the batches. There should be about 3 or 4 batches. Strain the puree through a fine-mesh sieve or a colander lined with triple-layered cheesecloth. Transfer the soup base to an airtight container and chill in the refrigerator until ready to use.

In a medium-size pot, cook the remaining ¼ cup lentils in the remaining 1 cup stock with a pinch of salt and the lemon peel, simmering until tender but not mushy, about 20 minutes. Let cool, then drain the lentils and remove and discard the lemon peel.

In a large stockpot, heat the soup base over medium-low heat, being careful not to let it burn. Season with salt and pepper.

In a large sauté pan over medium-high heat, melt the butter until it begins to brown lightly and becomes fragrant, about 1 minute. Stir in the lobster meat and drained lentils; remove from the heat and stir in the lemon juice.

Divide the bisque into individual soup bowls and spoon the lobster mixture into the center of each serving. Serve with the bread.

2 cups heavy cream

Kosher salt

1 (3-inch) piece lemon peel

Freshly ground black pepper

¼ cup unsalted butter

1 teaspoon freshly squeezed lemon juice

1 loaf Rustic Bread (page 230), warmed and sliced

SUGAR PUMPKIN SALAD
WITH WHIPPED RICOTTA, TOASTED SEEDS & CURRY OIL

Sugar pumpkins are the small ones that appear at farmers' markets and farmstands in early fall. Add creamy ricotta and bitter frisée, plus the floral aroma and spice of cardamom and chiles, and you've got one beautiful dish.

SERVES 4

- 2 teaspoons curry powder
- 6 tablespoons extra-virgin olive oil
- 1 small sugar pumpkin
- Kosher salt and freshly ground black pepper
- 2 tablespoons unsalted butter
- ¼ teaspoon ground cardamom
- 1 cup ricotta cheese
- ¼ cup heavy cream
- ½ teaspoon chile flakes
- 1 head frisée lettuce, root end removed, leaves washed
- 2 teaspoons freshly squeezed lemon juice

Toast the curry powder in a small dry sauté pan until just fragrant. Add 3 tablespoons of the oil and heat until just warmed. Let the curried oil sit at room temperature for at least 1 hour, and refrigerate in an airtight container until ready to use. Mix well before serving.

Preheat the oven to 350°F. Line a baking sheet with foil.

Trim the top and bottom off of the pumpkin and peel with a vegetable peeler. Cut the pumpkin in half from top to bottom and remove and save the seeds. Rinse off the seeds and let them dry on paper towels. Cut each half of the pumpkin into thirds and then into ½-inch chunks. Toss the chunks with 2 tablespoons of the oil and place on the prepared baking sheet. Season with salt and pepper and bake for 15 to 20 minutes, until the chunks are soft enough to pierce with a skewer, but not mushy. Let the pumpkin cool.

In a small saucepan, melt the butter and pour into a small bowl. Toss the butter with the pumpkin seeds and cardamom. Place the mixture on another foil-lined baking sheet; bake for 10 minutes.

In a stand mixer fitted with the paddle attachment, combine the ricotta, cream, chile flakes, and salt and pepper to taste, and mix for 20 seconds (or, if using a wooden spoon, for 1 minute). The mixture should be light and creamy.

Spread the ricotta on individual serving plates in a thin layer. Place a few chunks of pumpkin on top of the ricotta. Toss the frisée with the remaining 1 tablespoon oil and the lemon juice, and put a small tuft on top of the pumpkin. Sprinkle the toasted seeds over the frisée and drizzle the curry oil around the salad. Serve at once.

MAINE
BEER COMPANY

Freeport, Maine
David and Daniel Kleban

Like so many New England brewers, brothers David and Daniel Kleban got their start by brewing beer at home. It was a passion Daniel discovered while in law school in 2007. He was interning at a law firm when an attorney from the firm gave him a home-brewing demo—he immediately took a shine to the process. When they eventually launched Maine Beer Company with a hoppy, California-style India pale ale (IPA) called Peeper in 2010, the Kleban brothers were one of the first "nano-breweries" in the country. The term, which describes breweries using one- to three-barrel systems, had barely been coined.

The two might have started small, but their beers caught on quickly. "We were trying to make IPAs and pale ales and would brew all kinds of stuff that we like to drink," says David. At the time, it was hard to get West Coast IPAs in Maine, but Daniel managed to perfect the style. They quickly expanded from their small, one-barrel home system to fifteen barrels. By 2011 they'd installed a second fermenter (they worked out of a multi-unit industrial park) and launched beers like Zoe, an amber; Mean Old Tom, an intense, vanilla-scented stout; and Lunch, a West Coast–style IPA.

Today, the brothers employ about a dozen people, with Daniel in charge of brewing the beers and David handling the business. Daniel has scratched the law gig to brew full time, and they've moved their brewery to Freeport, where they now have a tasting room and the capacity to brew more than six thousand barrels a year. "We're not going to be a big brewery," says David, who still dabbles in the financial world. "We'll do beers that we like and do them really well."

Altogether, they brew six beers on a regular rotation, along with a few seasonals throughout the year. And like so many other brewers at nano- and micro-sized operations in the area, they're partnering with others on special bottlings, like the anniversary project they released in fall 2013, which was created with fellow Portland brewers at Allagash Brewing and Eric Michaud, owner of the local *biergarten* Novare Res. Says David, "Three years in, it seems we've found our niche."

LINE-CAUGHT SWORDFISH

WITH CRISP BRUSSELS SPROUT LEAVES

Swordfish come through New England in the fall when they're following the Gulf Stream. Try to source local swordfish for this dish. Look for firm pieces that have no odor and a dry appearance. Crisping up Brussels sprout leaves is one of those easy tricks that adds both color and texture to an otherwise basic dish.

SERVES 4

12 Brussels sprouts

3 cups canola oil

Kosher salt

4 (8-ounce) swordfish steaks, about 2 inches thick

Freshly ground black pepper

Juice of 1 lemon

Preheat the oven to 350°F.

Cut the root end off the Brussels sprouts and carefully peel away the leaves and separate them (it might take several cuts off the bottom to accomplish this). Remove the leaves until you get down to the core; discard the core. The Brussels sprouts can be prepared to this point well ahead of time but should be cooked just before serving.

To cook the leaves, heat 2¾ cups of the oil in a deep medium-size saucepan to 350°F on a deep-frying thermometer. Carefully fry about half of the leaves until they're crisp and the edges are browned, about 45 seconds. (When adding the leaves, the oil will bubble up, and so be sure to use a high-sided pot and a long-handled slotted spoon.) Transfer the crisp leaves to a paper towel to drain; immediately sprinkle with salt before frying the second batch.

In a large oven-safe sauté pan, heat the remaining ¼ cup oil over medium-high heat. Season the swordfish with salt and pepper and sear on one side until golden brown, about 4 minutes. Flip it over and transfer the pan to the oven. Bake for 5 minutes to finish cooking.

Remove the fish to a paper towel to drain. Drizzle lemon juice over the fish. Place on individual plates, and pile the crisp sprout leaves on top. Serve warm.

Serve with Cauliflower with Brown Butter and Thyme (page 146).

LOBSTER CASSEROLE

This updated version of a traditional recipe is a nod to all the New England grandmothers out there who have been making their own lobster casseroles for years. I include it on my Thanksgiving table, as it's a great holiday dish for sharing with friends and family.

Preheat the oven to 375°F.

Steam the lobsters for 4 minutes (see page 239), then plunge them into ice water to stop the cooking. The lobsters will be undercooked but cooked enough to remove the meat from the shells. Remove the meat and cut it into 1-inch pieces; you should have about 2½ cups lobster meat. Save the small legs on the underside of the lobsters for the sauce.

In a large stockpot, heat the oil over medium heat. Add the leeks, potatoes, legs from the cooked lobster, celery root trimmings, and parsnip trimmings. Sweat the mixture for 5 minutes, then add the sherry and bring to a boil. Add the stock and simmer for 15 minutes. Add the cream and continue to simmer for 10 minutes.

In batches, transfer the mixture to a blender and puree until smooth, then strain through a fine-mesh sieve and discard the solids. Season with salt, pepper, and lemon juice; refrigerate in an airtight container until ready to use.

In a large nonstick pan, melt the butter and add the diced celery root, diced parsnip, carrot, and cauliflower florets; cook over medium heat until the vegetables begin to brown but are still slightly undercooked, 6 to 7 minutes. Cooking the vegetables may be done in two batches if your pan is not large enough. Remove the vegetables from the pan and place in a large bowl; let cool.

In the large bowl, mix the vegetables together with the lobster meat, parsley, and the sauce. Season the mixture with salt and pepper. Place the mixture in an 8-inch-square and 2-inch-deep baking dish. Top with the bread crumbs and bake until the mixture begins to brown and is bubbling, 15 to 20 minutes.

SERVES 6 TO 8

2 (1½-pound) lobsters

2 tablespoons canola oil

2 large leeks, white parts only, washed and sliced

2 large Yukon gold potatoes, peeled and cut into 2-inch pieces

1 small celery root, peeled and cut into 1-inch pieces; reserve the trimmings for the sauce

1 parsnip, peeled and cut into 1-inch pieces; reserve the trimmings for the sauce

½ cup dry sherry or brandy

2 cups Lobster Stock (page 219)

1 cup heavy cream

Kosher salt and freshly ground black pepper

1 tablespoon freshly squeezed lemon juice

4 tablespoons unsalted butter

1 carrot, diced

1 cup small cauliflower florets

2 tablespoons chopped fresh flat-leaf parsley

1 cup panko bread crumbs

SEARED SEA SCALLOPS

WITH CREAMY TURNIP PUREE & CRISP SHIITAKE MUSHROOMS

This dish combines a range of textures: the meaty bite of scallops, the smooth puree, and the crunch of crisp mushrooms. Use sea scallops, which are much larger than bay scallops and are usually sold by size, with codes like U10 or 20/30, which refer to the number of scallops per pound (U10 would be about 10 pieces per pound, and so on.) Make sure you are buying dry (phosphate-free) scallops from a trusted source. Pat the scallops dry with a paper towel to give them a better sear and don't season them until just before you put them into the pan.

SERVES 4

- 16 large shiitake mushrooms, stems removed
- ¼ cup plus 2 tablespoons canola oil
- 12 large sea scallops, about 1½ pounds
- Kosher salt and freshly ground white pepper
- 1 tablespoon freshly squeezed lemon juice
- Creamy Turnip Puree (recipe follows)
- 1 tablespoon thinly sliced chives

With a sharp knife, very thinly slice the mushrooms. In a medium sauté pan, heat ¼ cup of the oil over medium-high heat and sauté the mushrooms until crisp, about 8 minutes, shaking and stirring constantly so they don't burn. Remove the mushrooms to a paper towel to drain.

There should be about 2 tablespoons of oil left in the pan. Warm the remaining oil over medium-high heat until it starts to smoke lightly. Season half of the scallops with salt and white pepper. Place the seasoned half in the oil (make sure the pan isn't crowded). When the scallops are golden brown and release easily from the pan, about 1 to 2 minutes, flip them over and remove the pan from the heat. Let the scallops sit in the pan off the heat for 1 minute. Transfer the scallops to a serving plate and drizzle with lemon juice. Wipe out the pan and add the remaining 2 tablespoons oil. Season and cook the second batch of scallops the same way.

Spoon ¼ cup of the turnip puree on each of four individual plates. Top with the scallops and garnish with chives and the crisp shiitakes, and the reserved turnips from the puree.

CREAMY TURNIP PUREE

In a medium saucepan, heat the oil over medium heat, add the shallot, and sauté until it begins to color lightly, 3 to 4 minutes. Add the wine and simmer until the liquid is almost completely reduced. Add the turnips and cream and simmer until the turnips are tender but not falling apart, about 8 to 10 minutes.

Remove from the heat and let cool in the pan for 5 minutes. Set aside ¼ cup turnips for use as garnish. Transfer to a blender, along with the stock, and puree until smooth. Season with salt and pepper.

1 tablespoon canola oil

1 shallot, sliced

¼ cup white wine

2 scarlet or regular turnips, peeled and cut into 1-inch pieces

¾ cup heavy cream

½ cup Vegetable Stock (page 220)

Kosher salt and freshly ground black pepper

SPICED SKATE WING

Skate might seem like an unusual choice for the home cook, but it has a nice firm texture and a really sweet flavor. Here, I toss it with a seasoned flour and quickly sauté it for an easy weeknight dish. Buy skate from a trusted fishmonger and give it a sniff before bringing it home (it takes on an ammonia smell when beginning to go bad). If you can't find skate, freshwater trout is a great substitute, but it might require a minute or two longer to cook, depending on the thickness.

4 tablespoons extra-virgin olive oil

1 garlic clove, crushed

2 tablespoons freshly squeezed lemon juice

1 cup all-purpose flour

1 teaspoon ground cumin

1 tablespoon dry mustard

1 tablespoon ground turmeric

1 teaspoon freshly ground white pepper

1 teaspoon ground coriander

1 teaspoon curry powder

4 tablespoons canola oil

4 (6-ounce) skate wing fillets, trimmed, skin removed

Kosher salt and freshly ground black pepper

In a small sauté pan, heat the olive oil and garlic over medium heat until the garlic starts to brown just a little, about 3 minutes. Remove from the heat and place in a small bowl. Let cool for 1 hour. Just before serving, whisk the lemon juice into the garlic oil.

In a large bowl, combine the flour with the cumin, dry mustard, turmeric, white pepper, coriander, and curry powder. Set aside.

In a cast-iron skillet or large sauté pan, heat 2 tablespoons of the canola oil over medium-high heat.

Dredge the skate in the flour mixture and shake off any excess. Season the fish with salt and black pepper. Place two pieces of fish in the pan and cook until they begin to brown lightly, 1 to 2 minutes. Flip over the fish and immediately remove the pan from the heat; let the fish rest in the pan for 30 seconds before removing it. Repeat with the remaining 2 tablespoons oil and the remaining fillets.

Place the fillets on individual plates. Drizzle with garlic oil just before serving.

Serve with Toasted Orzo with Spinach and Chorizo (page 149).

SLOW-ROASTED TURKEY

WITH SIMPLE GRAVY

When it comes to cooking turkey, I take a traditional approach. This simple recipe will give you a great-tasting bird every time. Spend the extra money for a quality bird from a local farm, and you'll really taste the difference.

SERVES 8 TO 10

1 (12-pound) turkey, innards removed, wings removed and reserved for the gravy below

1 recipe (about 1 gallon) Brine (page 221)

2 sprigs fresh rosemary

2 garlic cloves, crushed

½ cup (1 stick) unsalted butter

6 fresh sage leaves

Kosher salt and freshly ground black pepper

Simple Gravy (recipe follows)

In a container large enough to hold the turkey snugly, pour the brine over the bird and let sit for at least 2 hours or up to 6 hours. (If brining longer than 2 hours, place the container in the refrigerator. Bring the turkey to room temperature before roasting.) Drain the turkey well and pat it dry. Discard the brine.

Preheat the oven to 450°F.

Fill the turkey breast cavity with the rosemary and garlic and truss the turkey (see page 179). Place it on a roasting rack in a roasting pan. Melt the butter with the sage leaves and brush it all over the outside of the turkey. Season the turkey aggressively with salt and pepper and place it in the oven.

Roast the turkey for 5 minutes, then rotate the pan 180 degrees and cook for another 5 minutes. Brush the outside with more of the sage butter and lower the oven temperature to 300°F. Roast for 90 more minutes; every 20 minutes or so, brush a little more butter on the turkey. Check the internal temperature with a meat thermometer and remove from the oven when the thickest part of the breast meat registers 155°F. Cover loosely with foil and let rest for 30 minutes.

To serve, slice the turkey breast off by cutting down the middle of the backbone, starting with the blade against the bone. Remove both breasts from the rib cage, doing your best to keep the skin intact. Cut both breasts into slices and arrange on a large platter. Remove the legs, separate the thighs and drumsticks, and place on the platter. Serve with the gravy alongside.

RECIPE CONTINUES

SIMPLE GRAVY

MAKES ABOUT 2 CUPS

¼ cup canola oil

2 wings from the turkey

1 large shallot, thinly sliced

¼ cup unsalted butter

¼ cup all-purpose flour

3 cups Chicken Stock (page 219)

2 sprigs fresh thyme

2 bay leaves

Kosher salt and freshly ground black pepper

1 teaspoon sherry vinegar

In a large heavy saucepan, heat the oil over medium-high heat. Add the turkey wings and cook until they start to brown, about 4 minutes per side. Add the shallot and sauté until it begins to color, another 4 to 5 minutes. Remove from the heat and drain off any excess fat. Transfer the wings and shallot to a plate. In the same pan, melt the butter and stir in the flour; scrape the bottom of the pan so that it doesn't burn. Whisk in the stock and keep whisking until it comes to a simmer; add the cooked wings, shallots, thyme, and bay leaves. Lower the heat and simmer gently for 30 minutes, stirring frequently to keep the gravy from burning.

Remove from the heat, strain through a fine-mesh sieve, and discard the solids. Season with salt, pepper, and vinegar. Serve warm or refrigerate in an airtight container until ready to use (rewarm in a clean saucepan over medium-low heat, stirring frequently).

GRILLED NEW YORK STRIP STEAK

WITH MUSHROOMS IN RED WINE SAUCE

Every home cook should have a solid steak recipe in their repertoire. This one, which uses a strip steak, includes a simple but elegant red wine sauce with mushrooms. Blue Cheese Croquettes (page 115) on the side bring the steak to the next level, but you also can't go wrong with Scallion Whipped Potatoes (page 225).

In a large sauté pan over medium-high heat, melt the butter; as soon as it's melted, add the mushrooms. Cook until the mushrooms and the butter begin to brown, about 6 minutes. Lower the heat to medium and stir in the shallots. Continue to cook until the shallots become translucent, 3 to 4 minutes. Remove from the heat and drain off any excess fat from the pan. Add the wine sauce and let simmer for 4 minutes. Turn off the heat and let the mushroom sauce sit at room temperature until ready to use. Season with salt and pepper, if needed.

Preheat the oven to 300°F.

Season the steak very well with salt and pepper. In an oven-safe sauté pan that is large enough to hold all four steaks, heat the oil over medium-high heat. Add the steaks and sear well on both sides, about 3 minutes per side. Remove the pan from the heat and place the garlic and thyme on top of the steaks.

Put the pan in the oven and bake for 6 minutes for medium-rare. Remove the pan from the oven and let the steaks rest in the pan for 5 minutes before serving.

While the steaks are cooking, warm the mushroom sauce. When the steaks are ready, remove them from the oven and discard the garlic and thyme. Place the steaks in the center of a serving platter. Carefully spoon the mushrooms over each steak, letting the sauce spill over (most of the mushrooms should remain on top of the steaks). Garnish with parsley and blue cheese.

Serve with Blue Cheese Croquettes (page 115).

RECIPE CONTINUES

SERVES 4

- ¼ cup unsalted butter
- 4 ounces (about 3 cups) cremini mushrooms, washed, stems removed, cut in half
- 2 large shallots, thinly sliced
- 1 cup Red Wine Sauce (recipe follows)
- Kosher salt and freshly ground black pepper
- 4 (10-ounce) center-cut strip steaks from a small sirloin, about 2 inches thick
- ¼ cup canola oil
- 4 large garlic cloves, crushed
- 4 sprigs fresh thyme
- 2 tablespoons chopped fresh flat-leaf parsley
- 2 tablespoons crumbled blue cheese

RECIPE CONTINUED

RED WINE SAUCE

In a large saucepan, heat the oil over medium heat and add the shallot. Cook until the shallot just starts to brown, about 4 minutes. Increase the heat to medium-high and add the garlic and mushrooms; cook until most of the moisture is cooked out of the mushrooms, 3 to 4 minutes. Pour any excess oil out of the pan and add the wine; simmer until the wine is reduced by half, about 7 minutes. Add the stock, thyme, peppercorns, and sage leaves. Simmer until the liquid has reduced to a little more than 1 cup, about 15 minutes. Strain through a fine-mesh sieve into a clean small saucepan.

Just before serving, bring the sauce back to a simmer; stir in the vinegar. Remove from the heat, whisk in the butter, and season with salt and pepper.

MAKES ABOUT 1 CUP

3 tablespoons canola oil

1 shallot, sliced

1 garlic clove, smashed

¼ cup chopped cremini mushrooms

1 cup red wine

4 cups Veal Stock (page 220)

2 sprigs fresh thyme

5 whole black peppercorns

2 fresh sage leaves

1 teaspoon sherry vinegar

1 tablespoon unsalted butter

Kosher salt and freshly ground black pepper

MAPLE-BRINED PORK RACK
WITH APPLES & LEEKS

It's easier to buy quality pork than ever before. Small farms are introducing new breeds, which means you don't have to rely on feedlot-grown, mass-produced pork. In New England, meat CSAs from local family farms have become popular, especially since they offer buyers an opportunity to taste something that was raised humanely. As there are only two racks per animal, small farms might not have many to offer. Be sure to place an advance request with your local butcher before making this flavorful fall recipe. If you can't get a rack, you can also use this preparation on a shoulder or leg.

SERVES 8

8 cups warm water

1½ cups kosher salt, plus more to taste

½ cup brown sugar

2 sprigs fresh thyme

1 teaspoon whole black peppercorns

2 bay leaves

2 garlic cloves, crushed

1 teaspoon chile flakes

1 cup ice

1 (8-bone) pork rack

Freshly ground black pepper

1 sprig fresh rosemary

¼ cup unsalted butter

2 large Granny Smith apples, peeled and cored, cut into 8 pieces each

INGREDIENTS CONTINUE

In a bowl that's large enough to hold the pork rack, combine the warm water with the 1½ cups salt and the brown sugar; stir until dissolved. Add the thyme, peppercorns, bay leaves, garlic, chile flakes, and ice and stir to combine. Place the pork rack in the brine and let sit at room temperature, uncovered, for 30 to 40 minutes. Remove and pat dry. Reserve the sprig of thyme.

Preheat the oven to 450°F.

Place the pork on a roasting rack and season liberally with salt and ground pepper. Place the thyme (leftover from the brine) and rosemary sprigs on top of the pork. Roast for 15 minutes. Lower the heat to 325°F and continue roasting for about 1 hour and 15 minutes, or until the internal temperature reaches 135°F. Let the meat rest for 20 minutes before slicing.

While the pork is resting, warm the butter over medium heat in a large sauté pan until it begins to brown lightly. Stir in the apples and cook until they begin to color, 5 to 6 minutes. Add the leeks and cook until they begin to wilt and color lightly, another 3 minutes. Off the heat, pour in the Bourbon, then return to medium heat. Boil the Bourbon down until there is less than 1 tablespoon left in the pan. Add the stock and simmer for about 3 minutes, until the mixture thickens slightly. Season with salt and pepper; stir in the parsley.

Slice the pork rack into portions by cutting between the bones; this will give you 8 servings. Place each piece of pork in the center of an individual plate and spoon the apple mixture over the top. Serve immediately.

1 large leek, cut in half lengthwise, washed, then thinly sliced crosswise

3 tablespoons Bourbon

¼ cup Chicken Stock (page 219)

2 tablespoons chopped fresh flat-leaf parsley

SAGE & FENNEL– STUFFED ROASTED LEG OF LAMB

This comforting dish is a bit of a challenge to make at home but is well worth the effort. Try it a few times and you'll become an expert at tying lamb legs. The humblest cuts of lamb, like the leg, shank, and shoulder, can be the most flavorful. At Lineage, we roast lamb legs in the wood-burning oven and, they have one of the most soul-warming aromas.

SERVES 6 TO 8

1 large bulb fennel, top cut off

2 tablespoons canola oil

6 large fresh sage leaves, finely chopped, stems reserved

Grated zest of 1 lemon (about 1 packed tablespoon)

Kosher salt and freshly ground black pepper

1 (5- to 6-pound) lamb leg, bone removed

¼ cup extra-virgin olive oil

2 garlic cloves, thinly sliced

Core the fennel and cut it into ¼-inch pieces. In a large sauté pan, heat the canola oil over medium heat and add the fennel. Cook until it's just turning translucent, 5 to 6 minutes. Remove from the heat and add the sage and lemon zest. Season the filling with salt and pepper and let cool to room temperature.

While the fennel is cooling, unroll and lay the lamb leg flat so that the inside of the leg is exposed. Remove any large pieces of extra fat or sinew, and trim so that the meat is an even thickness. This might require cutting thicker pieces to butterfly them open or using a meat mallet to pound areas to make them thinner. The lamb should be 1 to 1½ inches thick.

Season the inside of the leg with salt and pepper and spread the fennel stuffing over the lamb, leaving about a 2-inch border around the edges. Carefully roll the lamb into a cylinder; the roast should be even all the way across. Using butcher's twine, tie the roast at 5 or 6 evenly spaced intervals.

Preheat the oven to 325°F.

In a small saucepan, heat the olive oil over medium heat; add the garlic and sage stems and cook until the garlic is lightly cooked, about 3 minutes. Remove from the heat and let cool to room temperature.

Place the lamb leg on a roasting rack and brush with the olive oil (let a couple of pieces of garlic and sage stick to the

outside). Season the outside of the leg liberally with salt and pepper and place in the oven. Roast for about 1 hour and 30 minutes. (The time may vary depending on the thickness and size of your roast.) Check the internal temperature with a meat thermometer; the center should read 140°F. Let the lamb rest for 20 minutes before slicing.

Serve with Roasted Onions (page 146) and Boiled Potatoes in Vegetable Stock (page 223).

ROASTED VENISON LOIN

Most deer consumed these days are raised on deer farms (there are several throughout New England), and the meat is spectacular. Venison is fairly lean but really rich in flavor. I rub the meat with a sweet, tangy mixture of honey and sherry vinegar in order to balance out that rich, gamey flavor. Try this recipe when you feel like experimenting—or when you or a neighbor has a freezer full of venison.

SERVES 6 TO 8

2 sprigs fresh rosemary, stemmed

1 garlic clove

1 teaspoon whole black peppercorns

¼ cup extra-virgin olive oil

1 tablespoon honey

1 teaspoon sherry vinegar

2 (2-pound) trimmed venison loins (reserve the trimmings for the Venison Sauce; recipe follows)

Kosher salt

½ cup Venison Sauce (recipe follows)

12 fresh flat-leaf parsley leaves

Mince the rosemary, garlic, and peppercorns together. In a small bowl, combine them with the oil, honey, and vinegar. Rub the mixture all over the venison and let marinate in the refrigerator for 1 hour.

Preheat the oven to 375°F.

Place the venison on a baking sheet and season liberally with salt. Roast for 10 minutes, then turn the heat down to 300°F and roast for an additional 40 minutes, or until the internal temperature reaches 140°F on a meat thermometer. Let the meat rest for about 20 minutes before slicing.

Slice the venison and shingle on a platter. Spoon the sauce around the meat; top with parsley leaves to garnish.

Serve with Macomber Turnip Gratin (page 193).

VENISON SAUCE

Venison trimmings and juniper berries add a depth of flavor and floral notes to this sauce. If you don't have these ingredients, Chicken Sauce (page 181) makes a great alternative.

Heat the oil in a medium saucepan over medium-high heat; add the shallots and venison trimmings. Cook until they begin to brown, about 4 minutes, stirring frequently. Remove from the heat and pour off any excess oil. Add the wine and return to medium-high heat; simmer until the wine has reduced by half. Add the stock, juniper berries (if using), peppercorns, and thyme; simmer gently until the liquid has reduced to 1 cup, about 30 minutes.

If you're making the sauce in advance, strain through a fine-mesh sieve and refrigerate in an airtight container until ready to use, up to 4 days. Just before using the sauce, transfer to a small saucepan and bring to a simmer. Add the vinegar and whisk in the butter. Lower the heat to low so that the sauce doesn't boil after you've added the butter. Season with salt and serve warm.

MAKES ABOUT 1 CUP

3 tablespoons canola oil

2 shallots, thinly sliced

2 or 3 pieces venison trimmings from the loin (½ to 1 cup)

1 cup red wine

4 cups Dark Chicken Stock (page 219)

2 dry juniper berries (optional)

3 whole black peppercorns

2 sprigs fresh thyme

1 teaspoon sherry vinegar

2 tablespoons unsalted butter

Kosher salt

HAND-ROLLED POTATO GNOCCHI

WITH ROASTED CHESTNUT PUREE & WILD MUSHROOMS

Gnocchi take time and patience to master. They may not come out perfectly the first time you attempt to make them. The size of the potato, moisture content, and temperature of the dough have an impact on the results. If you can't find fresh chestnuts, frozen ones will work for the puree.

SERVES 4

- 5 large Idaho potatoes
- 1 to 2 cups kosher salt (if baking the potatoes; otherwise salt to taste)
- 7 tablespoons unsalted butter
- 3 large egg yolks
- 1 whole large egg
- Freshly ground black pepper
- 1½ to 2 cups all-purpose flour, plus extra for dusting
- 2 tablespoons canola oil
- 2 cups wild mushrooms, cleaned and patted dry, cut the same size as the gnocchi
- 1 teaspoon sherry vinegar
- Chestnut Puree (recipe follows), warm
- 3 tablespoons grated pecorino cheese
- 2 tablespoons finely chopped fresh chives

If using a food mill: Preheat the oven to 350°F. With a paring knife, carefully stab the outside of each potato about 20 times. Place the potatoes on a bed of kosher salt on a baking sheet and bake for 1½ hours. The potato skin should be a little crisp, and the flesh in the middle cooked through. Remove the potatoes from the oven and cut them in half; let cool for a few minutes, then scoop out the flesh of the potato and put through a food mill into a mixing bowl. The milled potato should be fluffy and dry in appearance.

If using a grater: Peel the potatoes and cut them into quarters. Put them in a pot filled with cold salted water and bring to a boil; let simmer until they are just tender, but not mushy, about 15 minutes. Drain, let cool slightly, then grate the potatoes with a box grater or Microplane Zester. Discard any large pieces of potato mixed in with the grated pieces. The smaller and more uniform the potato, the smoother the resulting gnocchi dough. Spread the grated potato out on a baking sheet and bake for 5 to 10 minutes, until the potato is dry and fluffy.

In a small sauté pan over medium heat, melt 3 tablespoons of the butter until it becomes frothy, browned, and fragrant, about 4 minutes. Let cool slightly.

Place the milled or grated potato in a large bowl and, using a spatula, stir in the brown butter, egg yolks, and whole egg.

Season with salt and pepper, then start adding the flour ¼ cup at a time, incorporating each addition thoroughly before adding more. Add enough flour to make the dough dry enough to handle. Place on a work surface and fold in the remaining flour by hand until the dough is moist but not sticky; how much flour you use will depend on how wet your dough is. Do not overwork the dough.

Cut the dough into four equal pieces. Roll each piece into a long, ropelike shape; cut into 1-inch pillow-shaped pieces. Place on a floured baking sheet and refrigerate. The gnocchi may be stored in the refrigerator covered with plastic wrap for 1 day, or in an airtight container in the freezer for up to 2 weeks.

RECIPE CONTINUES

Bring a large pot of salted water to a rolling boil and carefully drop in the gnocchi. Keep the water at a simmer and cook until the gnocchi float to the top. Remove with a slotted spoon and place in a bowl of ice water until chilled.

In a large sauté pan, heat the oil over medium-high heat and add the mushrooms. Cook until they begin to color, 3 to 4 minutes, then add the remaining 4 tablespoons of butter and the cooled gnocchi. Sauté until the gnocchi begin to brown lightly, coating them in the butter, 4 to 5 minutes. Remove from the heat and drain off the excess fat from the pan. Season with salt, pepper, and vinegar.

Spread a few tablespoons of the warm Chestnut Puree on a large, shallow serving platter or four individual serving bowls. Spoon the gnocchi and mushroom mixture over the puree; top with pecorino cheese and chives and serve at once.

CHESTNUT PUREE

MAKES ABOUT 2 CUPS

12 large fresh chestnuts

3 tablespoons unsalted butter

1 large shallot, sliced

2 cups heavy cream

2 large fresh sage leaves

1 cup Vegetable Stock (page 219)

Kosher salt and freshly ground black pepper

1 tablespoon freshly squeezed lemon juice

Preheat the oven to 350°F.

Score the outside of the chestnut shells with a paring knife and roast for 2 minutes. The shell will begin to pull back from where it was scored. Let rest until cool enough to handle but still warm. (The cooler they get, the harder they are to peel.) Peel, then slice each chestnut into 3 or 4 pieces.

In a large saucepan, heat the butter over medium heat until it begins to brown, about 4 minutes. Add the chestnuts and cook until they start to brown, about 3 minutes. Add the shallot and cook for 30 seconds. Add the cream and sage and simmer for 10 minutes. Remove from the heat and let cool slightly.

Puree the chestnut mixture in a blender until smooth, using the stock to thin as needed (you may not need to use the whole cup). Pour through a fine-mesh sieve and season with salt, pepper, and lemon juice. Keep warm in a bowl covered with plastic wrap until ready to use. The puree will thicken as it cools, and so add a little more stock before serving.

ROASTED BRUSSELS SPROUTS

Not everyone is a fan of Brussels sprouts, which is why I like to add bacon to this dish. It's hard not to love a dish that includes bacon. Don't be afraid to increase the roasting time if necessary: A little color on the outside leaves improves the flavor. Brussels sprouts were originally cultivated in Brussels, Belgium, but started being grown in the United States in the eighteenth century. The plants thrive in New England during the cool fall months.

Preheat the oven to 400°F.

Trim the root ends off the sprouts and pull off any discolored leaves. Fill a large bowl with ice water. In a medium saucepan, bring 2 quarts water and the salt to a boil. Add the Brussels sprouts to the boiling water and simmer for 30 seconds. Drain and plunge the Brussels sprouts into the ice water to stop the cooking. When cool, drain well.

Cut the sprouts in half from top to bottom. Toss with the melted butter and spread on a baking sheet; season with salt and white pepper. Roast for 20 to 25 minutes.

Meanwhile, heat the oil in a large sauté pan over medium heat. Sauté the shallots until they are colored lightly, 4 to 5 minutes. Pull the Brussels sprouts out of the oven and add them to the shallots; toss together, then season with lemon juice, salt, and white pepper. Sprinkle pecorino over the top. Serve immediately.

VARIATION

Remove the skin from 10 ounces Slab Bacon (page 242) and cut the bacon into 1-inch-long, ¼-inch-thick lardons. While the Brussels sprouts are roasting, heat the oil in a sauté pan over medium-high heat. Add the bacon and cook until it begins to crisp, about 5 minutes. Add the shallots and cook until the shallots start to color slightly, another 2 to 3 minutes. Pour all but 1 tablespoon of fat from the pan before adding the roasted Brussels sprouts.

SERVES 4

2 pounds Brussels sprouts

3 tablespoons kosher salt, plus more to taste

½ cup (1 stick) unsalted butter, melted

Freshly ground white pepper

1 tablespoon canola oil

2 shallots, sliced

2 tablespoons freshly squeezed lemon juice

2 tablespoons grated pecorino

ROASTED ONIONS

Roasting onions is a great way to bring out their sweetness. This side pairs well with a number of fall main dishes, and is convenient for larger meals because it can be made a day or two in advance. I use red onions, but sweet white onions are a good substitute.

SERVES 6 TO 8

4 large red onions, peeled

Extra-virgin olive oil

Kosher salt and freshly ground black pepper

Preheat the oven to 350°F.

Cut the onions in half lengthwise and remove the root end. Cut the halves into thick wedges and toss with just enough oil to coat the onions; season with salt and pepper.

Put the onion wedges on a baking sheet and roast for 30 minutes, or until the edges become browned and crisp. Serve warm; or let cool, refrigerate in an airtight container for up to 2 days, and reheat in a warm oven.

CAULIFLOWER
WITH BROWN BUTTER & THYME

Cauliflower is a very versatile vegetable—it can be easily made into a soup or a puree, or just roasted like it is in this simple dish. Let the florets really brown with the butter to enhance the amazing nutty flavor. The lemon zest helps cut through some of the richness.

SERVES 4

½ cup (1 stick) unsalted butter

1 head cauliflower, cored, cut into florets

2 teaspoons fresh thyme leaves

Kosher salt and freshly ground black pepper

½ teaspoon grated lemon zest

In a large sauté pan, melt the butter over medium heat until it just begins to bubble. Add the cauliflower florets and cook until they begin to brown, about 8 minutes, stirring frequently so they cook evenly. Drain off any excess butter. Add the thyme leaves, then season with salt, pepper, and lemon zest. Serve hot.

VEGETABLE HASH

This is a great side dish for the holiday season. It's relatively easy to prepare and looks beautiful on the table. The brown butter adds a great nutty flavor that brings out the earthiness of these classic fall vegetables.

Preheat the oven to 350°F.

Cut the potatoes lengthwise into quarters and, in a roasting pan, toss them with the oil and sage. Roast for 20 minutes, or until they begin to brown lightly. Let cool.

In a large nonstick sauté pan, melt the butter over medium heat and cook until it begins to brown. Add the squash, pumpkin, and parsnips. Cook over medium heat until they begin to brown and soften, about 10 minutes. Stir in the shallots and garlic and sauté for 2 more minutes. (If the garlic and shallots begin to brown, turn down the heat.) Add the roasted potatoes, raisins (if using), and chard and stir frequently until the chard is wilted. Season with lemon zest and juice, salt, and pepper. Garnish with pumpkin seeds, if using. Serve immediately.

SERVES 8 TO 10

2 pounds fingerling potatoes, washed well

¼ cup extra-virgin olive oil

1 tablespoon chopped fresh sage

3 tablespoons unsalted butter

1 small acorn squash, peeled, seeded, and diced

1 sugar pumpkin, peeled, seeds removed (reserve the seeds for roasting), diced

4 parsnips, peeled and diced

3 shallots, thinly sliced

1 garlic clove, minced

1 cup golden raisins (optional)

2 cups red Swiss chard leaves (stems removed) cut into 2-inch strips

Grated zest and juice of 1 lemon

Kosher salt and freshly ground black pepper

Roasted Pumpkin Seeds (optional; page 227)

GLAZED SWEET POTATOES

The smell of glazed sweet potatoes makes me hungry and reminds me of fall's flavors. Don't buy potatoes that are too large; small- to medium-size ones are best in this dish.

8 tablespoons (1 stick) unsalted butter

¼ cup maple syrup

2 tablespoons brown sugar

¼ teaspoon freshly grated nutmeg

1 tablespoon red wine vinegar

¼ teaspoon ground cayenne

12 sweet potatoes, peeled and cut into 2-inch-thick rounds

Kosher salt and freshly ground black pepper

Preheat the oven to 375°F.

In a small saucepan over high heat, melt 6 tablespoons of the butter. Whisk in the maple syrup, brown sugar, nutmeg, vinegar, and cayenne and continue whisking until the mixture comes to a boil. Remove from the heat.

Using the remaining 2 tablespoons butter, grease a large baking dish. Place the sweet potato rounds in the prepared dish. Pour the butter mixture over the potatoes, then sprinkle with salt and pepper and cover tightly with foil. Bake for 50 minutes. Remove from the oven, uncover, and baste the potatoes with liquid from the pan. Bake uncovered for another 15 minutes. Remove from the oven and brush more of the liquid from the pan over the potatoes before serving.

TOASTED ORZO
WITH SPINACH & CHORIZO

I often pair this pasta dish with Spiced Skate Wing (page 127), but you can try it with other fish, chicken, or on its own. Chorizo is a spicy sausage that comes fresh or dry; for this recipe I use dry chorizo and cook it lightly. The heat from the sausage mellows when tossed with spinach and pasta.

Preheat the oven to 350°F.

Toss the orzo with the olive oil in a baking pan and toast in the oven for 7 minutes, stirring halfway through. The pasta should be lightly toasted and have a nutty smell to it.

Bring a large saucepan of salted water to a boil and add the toasted orzo, lower the heat, and simmer until tender, about 12 minutes. Drain and spread on a baking sheet to cool.

In a large sauté pan, heat the canola oil over medium-high heat and add the chorizo and onion. Sauté until some of the sausage fat starts to render out and the sausage begins to lightly crisp around the edges, about 6 minutes. Remove from the heat and drain off any excess fat. Add the orzo, lemon zest, and stock to the pan and warm through over medium heat. Add the spinach and immediately remove the pan from the heat; the spinach should be slightly wilted. Toss together and season with salt and pepper. Serve immediately.

SERVES 4

- 1 cup orzo pasta
- 1 tablespoon extra-virgin olive oil
- Kosher salt
- ¼ cup canola oil
- 6 ounces dry chorizo sausage, cut into thin rounds
- 1 red onion, cut in half lengthwise and then into ¼-inch-wide strips
- 1 teaspoon grated lemon zest
- 3 tablespoons Vegetable Stock (page 220)
- 2 cups lightly packed baby spinach
- Freshly ground black pepper

APPLE & POMEGRANATE STUFFING

The smell of a good stuffing brings back memories of my family's holiday dinners. Every family has their own recipe, one that's been made for years, with its own variations and ingredients. Stuffing can be heavy at a big meal and so my stuffing does not contain meat in order to keep it light. The apple and pomegranate make a nice complement to any roasted meat.

SERVES 10 (WITH LEFTOVERS)

- 1 loaf Cornbread (recipe follows), preferably day old
- 2 cups (4 sticks) unsalted butter, at room temperature
- 2 large Spanish onions, cut into ½-inch pieces
- 4 stalks celery, cut into ½-inch pieces
- 2 large carrots, cut into ½-inch pieces
- 3 tablespoons finely chopped fresh rosemary
- 2 Honeycrisp apples, peeled and cut into 1-inch pieces
- 2 tablespoons chopped fresh flat-leaf parsley
- Seeds from 1 pomegranate
- 4 cups Chicken Stock (page 219), at room temperature
- 6 large eggs
- Kosher salt and freshly ground black pepper

Cut cornbread into 2-inch pieces. (This should yield about 16 cups.) Let sit for 1 to 2 hours.

Preheat the oven to 350°F.

Melt 1½ cups (3 sticks) of the butter in a large sauté pan over medium heat. Add the onions, celery, and carrots and cook for 3 minutes. Stir in the rosemary and cook for another 1 minute. The vegetables should be just starting to soften but not completely cooked. Remove from the heat.

Put the bread in a large bowl and add the apple, parsley, pomegranate seeds, and 2 cups of the stock. Toss together, then add the vegetables and all of the butter from the pan to the bread mixture.

In a separate bowl, whisk together 1 cup of the stock and the eggs; fold into the bread mixture to coat. Season well with salt and pepper.

Using 2 tablespoons butter, grease a 13 by 9–inch baking dish, or one that is large enough to hold all of the stuffing. Pour the stuffing mixture into the dish; dot the remaining 6 tablespoons butter over the top and drizzle with the remaining 1 cup stock. Bake for 30 minutes, rotate the pan, then bake for an additional 30 minutes. Serve hot, straight from the baking dish, or refrigerate in an airtight container for up to 2 days, then let sit at room temperature for 1 hour before reheating.

CORNBREAD

Cornbread can be eaten on its own and also makes a great addition to many meals. The quality of the cornmeal will directly affect the outcome of the recipe.

Preheat the oven to 350°F. Using the butter, grease a 10 by 15–inch baking dish.

In a stand mixer fitted with the whisk attachment (or a large mixing bowl), whisk together the sugar, flour, cornmeal, baking soda, and salt.

In a separate bowl, whisk together the eggs, milk, and oil. Slowly whisk the wet ingredients into the dry until everything is incorporated.

Pour the batter into the prepared dish. Bake for 25 minutes, or until a knife inserted into the center comes out clean. Let the cornbread cool slightly before removing from the baking dish.

MAKES 1 (10 BY 15–INCH) LOAF

3 tablespoons unsalted butter, softened

¾ cup sugar

3 cups all-purpose flour

1 cup fine yellow cornmeal, such an Anson Mills

2 tablespoons baking soda

1 tablespoon kosher salt

3 large eggs

1¼ cups whole milk

¾ cup corn or canola oil

CRANBERRY CHUTNEY

I start making chutney as soon as cranberries are available. Besides being a wonderful Thanksgiving condiment, it is great spread on toast and sandwiches. Cranberries are one of just a few foods that are truly native to New England. An important resource to Native Americans, cranberries were also essential to settlers; the Cape Cod Cranberry Growers' Association was started in 1888.

Combine all the ingredients in a medium saucepan and simmer for 10 minutes or until the cranberries are very tender.

Run the mixture through a food mill, or blend in a blender, until smooth. Transfer to an airtight container and chill in the refrigerator until ready to use. Chutney will keep for 2 to 3 weeks. Serve cold.

MAKES ABOUT 2 CUPS

1 pound fresh cranberries

1 small red apple, cored and cut into 1-inch pieces

1 cup granulated sugar

½ cup freshly squeezed orange juice

Grated zest of 1 orange

¼ teaspoon ground cinnamon

¼ teaspoon ground turmeric

¼ teaspoon kosher salt

WINTER

While winter does not officially start until December 21st, we always feel the change in season well before that in New England. Farmers are planning and waiting for spring, and fishermen are fighting through the cold to try to scratch out a living during the toughest time of the year. However, there is a lot to look forward to, even in these bitter cold months.

I don't mind the snow or the cold weather. It's an opportunity for me to cook with big, hearty flavors and cuts of meat that taste just right for the season. Braised shanks, red wine, and grains all seem better this time of year. You may think lobsters are best in the summer, but they are hearty and delicious all winter long. When I was a teenager, I considered becoming a lobsterman; I spent several summers working on boats. Tan, strong, a few bucks in my pocket—it was pretty cool. But I was instantly cured of any misconceptions when my cousin Mark took me lobstering on a cold December day. The idea of spending long hours in a kitchen is more appealing to me than grinding it out on a boat in the dead of winter.

My grandmother's root cellar was always filled with homegrown squash and potatoes. How else could you make it through a New England winter but by preserving what you grew in the summer and fall? I remember my dad taking time off from work so that he could help with canning all the produce from the garden before the weather got too harsh.

New England farmers have gotten better at stretching the seasons to make sure greens are available earlier in the spring and to make others last longer into the year— but you cannot fool Mother Nature entirely. February is February, and spring is still a little while away, and so it's best to make the most of it. Braise a good cut of meat, enjoy some more winter squash, prepare rich and hearty soups.

Embrace the winter months like we do at my restaurants. Lineage has a fantastic wood-fired oven, and Eastern Standard invites guests in with its warm and festive ambiance. Light your own fireplace to create a comforting space. Celebrate the season with robust flavors of braises and roasts. Just think: Without winter, there would be no sledding, ice-skating, or skiing. So bundle up and enjoy the season's fun outdoor activities and the special culinary delights that go with it, like Maine shrimp and a hot bowl of soup. It won't last forever and always makes New Englanders feel like they've truly earned the first sunny day of spring.

WINTER

STARTERS

Fried Cod Cheeks WITH SPICY MAYONNAISE	155
Oysters Gregory WITH GRILLED LEEKS, BACON & PAPRIKA	157
Crisp Sweet Shrimp	158
Shrimp Salad WITH AVOCADO, GRAPEFRUIT & PICKLED RED ONION	160
Shrimp Risotto WITH BLOOD ORANGE	161
Pork Belly Confit WITH SWEET POTATO & SHIITAKE MUSHROOMS	162
Cauliflower Soup	165
Winter Baby Beet Salad WITH ORANGES, FRISÉE & PISTACHIOS	166

MAINS

Creamy Oyster Stew	171
Poached Winter Flounder	172
Pan-Roasted Hake	175
Baked Stuffed Lobster	176
Roasted Chicken	179
Updated Yankee Pot Roast	182
Roasted Duck Leg Confit	185
Simple Sausage & Beans	186
Braised Pork Shanks	189

SIDES

Rosemary Carrots	191
Savoy Cabbage WITH RED POTATOES & RUTABAGA	192
Macomber Turnip Gratin	193
Black Rice	194
Toasted Barley WITH CHANTENAY CARROTS & POMEGRANATE	195

FRIED COD CHEEKS
WITH SPICY MAYONNAISE

Fish cheeks are exactly what they sound like—they usually come from larger species like halibut, monkfish, and cod—and are a true delicacy. Turn to a good fishmonger to find them for you. Frying cod cheeks is a great way to use a part of the fish that might otherwise get tossed.

SERVES 4

- 1 pound cod cheeks, about the size of a quarter or a little larger
- ½ cup buttermilk
- ½ cup Homemade Mayonnaise (page 222)
- 2 tablespoons Sriracha hot sauce
- Kosher salt and freshly ground white pepper
- 1 lemon, cut into 8 wedges
- 1 quart canola oil
- 1 cup Seasoned Flour (page 158)
- 1 tablespoon finely chopped fresh rosemary (optional)

Separate the cheeks and trim off any small loose pieces that may be hanging from them. In a medium bowl, soak the cheeks in the buttermilk for 30 minutes.

In a small bowl, combine the mayonnaise and Sriracha, season with salt and pepper, and stir in the juice from two of the lemon wedges. Cover with plastic wrap and set aside.

In a large, heavy-bottom pot, heat the oil until it reaches 400°F on a deep-frying thermometer. Drain the excess liquid off the cheeks. Pour the flour into a shallow dish and, using your hands, toss the cheeks in the flour, coating them very well; shake off the excess flour and carefully place the cheeks in the hot oil. Working in batches, place the floured cheeks in the oil, making sure the temperature doesn't drop below 350°F, and cook for 60 seconds. Remove to a paper towel to drain. Sprinkle with rosemary (if using) and season with salt and white pepper.

Serve hot with the remaining lemon wedges and the mayonnaise on the side.

Serve with Hand-Cut Fries (page 225).

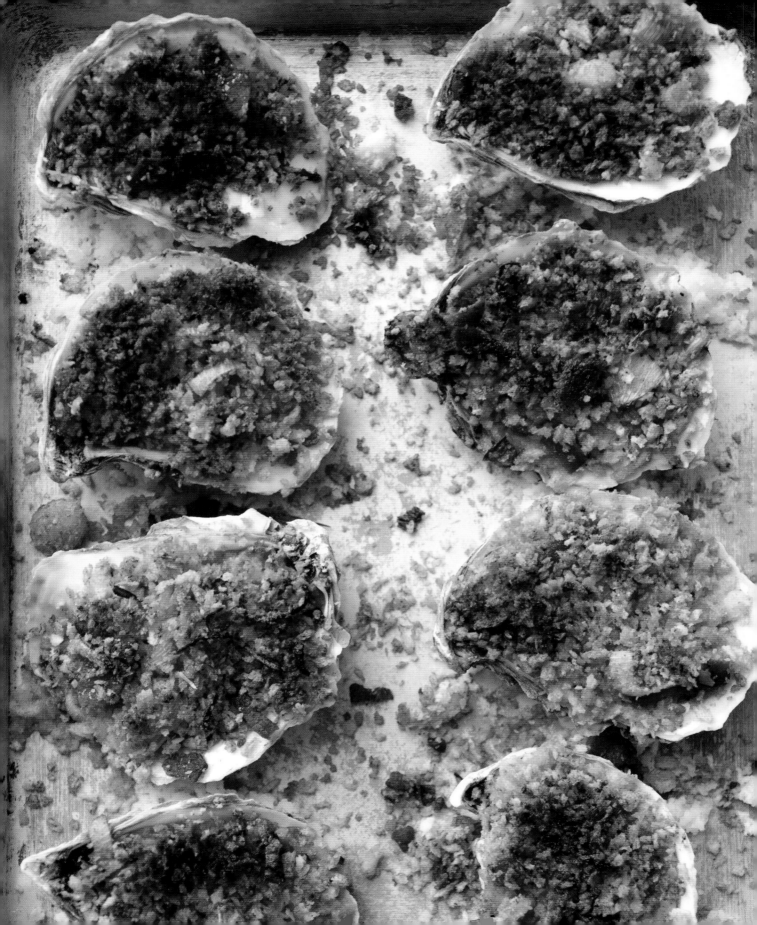

OYSTERS GREGORY
WITH GRILLED LEEKS, BACON & PAPRIKA

My good friend Shore Gregory, a partner at Island Creek Oyster Bar (ICOB) and Row 34, and I share a love of oysters. I cooked one of the first meals in the ICOB kitchen in honor of Shore's birthday and made these baked oysters. When I decided to put them on the menu, it only made sense to name them after him.

Shuck the oysters, saving the bottom shell and meat separately (see page 232). Clean out the shells and set aside. Refrigerate the oyster meat in a bowl, covered with plastic wrap, until ready to use.

Preheat a grill pan or sauté pan over medium-high heat. Brush the leek with a little bit of the oil and place both halves on the hot grill pan or sauté pan, flat side down. Grill for 1 minute, then roll it onto its side; repeat twice to grill all sides. The leek should not be fully cooked but have a little color from the grill pan ridges. Let cool slightly; slice into thin half circles.

In a sauté pan, heat the remaining oil over medium heat, add the bacon, and cook until it begins to brown, 4 to 5 minutes. Drain off all but 2 tablespoons of the fat and add the paprika, leeks, and garlic. Cook for 2 minutes over medium heat, stirring frequently, careful not to let the mixture burn. Remove from the heat and fold in the bread crumbs, tarragon, lemon zest, and lemon juice; season with salt and white pepper.

Preheat the oven to 400°F.

Mix a little water into 1 to 2 cups salt to make a paste. Mound the paste into a long, flat pedestal on a baking sheet. Place the cleaned oyster shells on top of the mound. Place an oyster in each shell and spoon the leek mixture over the oyster meat so that it is completely covered. Bake the oysters for 8 minutes, then turn on the broiler and cook for 2 more minutes.

To serve, create small mounds of salt paste on a large serving platter and place the baked oysters on top of the mounds.

MAKES 12 OYSTERS

12 large oysters

1 small leek, white part only, split lengthwise and washed

2 tablespoons canola oil

½ cup diced uncooked Slab Bacon (page 242)

1 tablespoon paprika

2 garlic cloves, minced

½ cup panko bread crumbs

1 tablespoon chopped fresh tarragon

1 teaspoon grated lemon zest

1 tablespoon freshly squeezed lemon juice

1 to 2 cups kosher salt for baking, plus more to taste

Freshly ground white pepper

CRISP SWEET SHRIMP

There are a lot of ways to cook Maine sweet shrimp, but nothing beats tossing them in batter and frying them up. The Maine shrimp season takes place in the dead of winter; most are caught by large draggers that scoop them up by the thousands. Since sweet shrimp are very perishable, they are usually sold canned or frozen. Some fishermen, like my cousin Mark, catch sweet shrimp in traps. There is a huge difference between shrimp that's been dragged and shrimp that's been trapped: The quality and size of trapped shrimp are always superior.

SERVES 4

½ cup buttermilk

2 teaspoons Tabasco sauce

1 pound peeled Maine sweet shrimp

1 quart canola oil

3 cups Seasoned Flour (recipe follows)

Kosher salt and freshly ground black pepper for seasoning

4 lemon wedges

½ cup Aïoli (page 222)

In a large bowl, combine the buttermilk and Tabasco sauce; add the shrimp, toss to coat it in the mixture, and refrigerate, covered with plastic wrap, for up to 1 hour.

Heat the oil in a large, heavy-bottom pot until it reaches 350°F on a deep-frying thermometer. Drain the excess liquid off the shrimp. Pour the flour into a shallow dish and, using your hands, toss the shrimp in the flour, coating them very well; shake off the excess flour and carefully place the shrimp in the hot oil. Fry for 45 to 60 seconds; they should be lightly browned and crisp. Remove the shrimp to a paper towel to drain; season with salt and pepper while hot. Serve immediately with lemon wedges and aïoli for dipping.

MAKES ABOUT 3 CUPS

3 cups all-purpose flour

1½ tablespoons dry mustard

1½ teaspoons ground turmeric

1½ teaspoons paprika

1½ teaspoons kosher salt

1½ teaspoons freshly ground white pepper

SEASONED FLOUR

In a large bowl, stir together the flour, dry mustard, turmeric, paprika, salt, and white pepper, making sure to combine thoroughly.

FOR THE SHRIMP

1 cup white wine

2 sprigs fresh thyme

1 bay leaf

1 lemon, cut in half

3 tablespoons kosher salt

1 garlic clove, crushed

1 pound Maine sweet shrimp, peel on but head removed

FOR THE SALAD

2 avocados

2 tablespoons freshly squeezed lemon juice

2 tablespoons extra-virgin olive oil

¼ cup Pickled Red Onion (recipe follows), roughly chopped

1 grapefruit, cut into segments (see page 166), with juice

1½ cups lightly packed baby arugula leaves

Kosher salt and freshly ground white pepper

SHRIMP SALAD
WITH AVOCADO, GRAPEFRUIT & PICKLED RED ONION

I like poaching shrimp in the shell to help keep its shape and color. If you have more shrimp than this simple salad calls for, use them in pasta or make a spicy shrimp salad for sandwiches.

Make the shrimp: In a large pot, combine 1 quart water, the wine, thyme, bay leaf, lemon, salt, and garlic and bring to a hard boil. Drop the shrimp into the pot and cook for 30 seconds.

Remove the shrimp with a slotted spoon to a platter so they can lay flat and cool to room temperature. Once cool, carefully peel the shrimp so they remain whole. Refrigerate in an airtight container for up to 2 days until ready to use.

Make the salad: Cut the avocados in half and remove the pits. Using a large spoon, remove the flesh. Cut the flesh into long slices and arrange them flat on a serving platter.

In a large mixing bowl, whisk together the lemon juice and oil. Add the shrimp, pickled onions, grapefruit, and arugula and toss together. Season with salt and white pepper. Carefully arrange the shrimp salad over the avocados and serve.

1 red onion, peeled

½ cup champagne vinegar

½ cup sugar

1 tablespoon kosher salt

PICKLED RED ONION

Cut the onion in half through the root end and remove any hard core or root. With a sharp knife, cut the onion into thin, crescent-shaped slices.

In a medium bowl, whisk together the vinegar, sugar, and salt; add the onion and let sit at room temperature for 1 hour, stirring every 20 minutes. Place the pickled onion in an airtight container and refrigerate for up to 4 days.

SHRIMP RISOTTO
WITH BLOOD ORANGE

The sweet, tart flavor of blood oranges goes well with shrimp, especially when paired with this creamy risotto. Be patient when making risotto: It takes time and care to get the consistency and seasonings just right.

In a large, heavy-bottom sauté pan, heat the canola oil over medium-high heat. Add the onion. Stir frequently, letting the onion cook until it becomes translucent but not browned, about 3 to 4 minutes. Stir in the rice and let toast for 1 minute, stirring frequently. Add the wine. Stir in 1 cup stock, incorporating any rice sticking to the sides of the pan. Lower heat to medium and let cook slowly, stirring every 10 seconds.

Once the stock has been absorbed and the rice begins to look dry, add another ½ cup stock. Stir constantly for about 2 to 3 minutes and continue to add another ½ cup of stock whenever the liquid is absorbed. Stir again for another 2 to 3 minutes. Each addition should take 2 to 3 minutes. The rice will begin to take on a creamy appearance.

When all of the stock has been incorporated, remove the pan from the heat. The rice should be creamy and tender but still a little al dente. Stir in the cream, lemon juice, and Parmesan; season with salt and pepper.

In a medium sauté pan, heat the butter over medium heat until it begins to brown lightly, about 3 minutes. Add the shrimp and cook until reheated, about 15 seconds. Add the blood orange segments and juice and stir to combine; remove from the heat.

Place the risotto in a serving bowl and spoon the shrimp and blood orange over the top. Garnish with parsley.

SERVES 4

2 tablespoons canola oil

½ cup minced Spanish onion

½ pound (about 1 cup) arborio rice

¾ cup white wine

4 cups Vegetable Stock (page 220), warm

½ cup heavy cream

1 tablespoon freshly squeezed lemon juice

2 tablespoons freshly grated Parmesan cheese

Kosher salt and freshly ground white pepper

1 tablespoon unsalted butter, softened

1 pound Maine sweet shrimp, cooked using same method as for Shrimp Salad (see page 160)

4 blood oranges, segmented (see page 166), juices reserved

1 tablespoon chopped fresh flat-leaf parsley

PORK BELLY CONFIT
WITH SWEET POTATO & SHIITAKE MUSHROOMS

Packed with flavor from the sweet potato and mushrooms, the Pork Belly Confit is a little rich, making it a treat on a winter day. It can be made a few days in advance and stored in fat until you're ready to serve it. Fresh pork belly is available from most good butchers.

SERVES 6

- 2½ pounds fresh pork belly
- 1 quart Brine (page 221)
- 3 cups duck fat, warmed until liquid
- 2 sprigs fresh rosemary
- 1 large sweet potato
- ¼ cup unsalted butter
- 1 cup heavy cream
- Kosher salt and freshly ground black pepper
- ¼ cup canola oil
- 18 shiitake mushrooms, stems removed, thinly sliced
- ¼ cup apple cider
- 1 cup Chicken Stock (page 219)
- 1 teaspoon sherry vinegar
- 2 tablespoons diced apple

Put the pork belly in a small container and pour the brine over it. Cover with plastic wrap and refrigerate for 4 to 6 hours (any longer and you run the risk of the belly becoming too salty).

Preheat the oven to 250°F.

Remove the belly from the brine and pat dry. Place the belly in a small baking dish so that it fits snugly. Pour the duck fat on top and add the rosemary. Bake for 3 to 5 hours. Start checking it after 3 hours; the belly should be easy to pierce with a sharp paring knife or skewer. Remove from the oven and let cool in the duck fat. When cool enough to handle, remove the belly from the fat and cut into 6 squares. The pork confit may be prepared to this point up to 5 days in advance. Refrigerate in an airtight container until ready to use.

Preheat the oven to 350°F.

Pierce the skin of the sweet potato with a paring knife several times and bake for 1 to 1½ hours, until cooked through. Remove from the oven and let cool slightly. (Lower the oven temperature to 300°F.) Cut the sweet potato in half lengthwise and scoop out the flesh; place in a food processor. Add the butter and pulse in the cream until the potato has a smooth, creamy texture; season with salt and pepper.

In a large sauté pan, heat the oil over high heat and add the mushrooms. Cook, stirring frequently, until the mushrooms begin to crisp, about 5 minutes. Pour the oil out of the pan and add the cider. Bring to a boil, then add the stock. Bring back to a boil, then lower the heat and simmer, stirring frequently, until there is about ½ cup liquid left in the pan, 15 to 20 minutes. Season with salt, pepper, and the vinegar.

Reheat the pork belly in the oven until warmed through; at the same time, warm up the sweet potato mixture and the mushrooms. To serve, place a spoonful of the sweet potato in the center of a serving platter; spoon the mushroom mixture around the potato; slice the warm pork belly and shingle the slices over the top of the sweet potato. Garnish with diced apple. Serve at once.

CAULIFLOWER SOUP

This satisfying winter soup is light but feels rich. Make it a day in advance so the flavors can deepen a bit.

Preheat the oven to 400°F.

In a small sauté pan, melt ¼ cup of the butter with 2 of the sage leaves over medium heat; be careful not to brown the butter.

Place the head of cauliflower on a baking sheet and brush the outside with the melted sage butter. Put the additional sage leaves on top of the cauliflower head; season with salt and white pepper and roast for 30 minutes. The cauliflower should have some color on the outside but will not be completely cooked through. Remove from the oven and let sit until cool enough to handle; reserve the sage leaves. Cut the cauliflower into 1-inch pieces.

In a large stockpot, heat the oil over medium heat. Add the leek, onion, and potato; sauté for 3 minutes, stirring frequently so that the vegetables don't color. Stir in the chopped cauliflower and roasted sage leaves, then add the stock. Bring the mixture to a simmer; add the thyme and bay leaf. Simmer for 20 minutes, or until the vegetables are almost tender. Add the cream and simmer for 10 more minutes. Remove from the heat and let cool slightly. Remove the bay leaf and thyme sprigs.

Puree the soup in a blender (this may take a few batches) until smooth. Strain the soup through a fine-mesh sieve; season with salt and white pepper. Return the soup to the pot.

Slowly warm the soup over low heat, stirring frequently so that it doesn't burn. In a small sauté pan, heat the remaining ¼ cup butter over medium heat until it begins to brown lightly, about 3 minutes. Add the remaining 6 sage leaves and cook for 10 seconds, until just crisp; remove from the heat.

Just before serving, season the soup with the lemon juice. Ladle the soup into individual bowls and pour the brown butter and sage leaves over the top of each serving.

MAKES ABOUT 2 QUARTS

½ cup (1 stick) unsalted butter

8 large fresh sage leaves

1 head cauliflower, green leaves removed, head intact, stem trimmed

Kosher salt and freshly ground white pepper

3 tablespoons canola oil

1 leek, white part only, split lengthwise and washed

1 small Spanish onion, peeled and cut into 1-inch pieces

1 Yukon gold potato, peeled and cut into 1-inch pieces

5 cups Vegetable Stock (page 220)

2 sprigs fresh thyme

1 fresh bay leaf

2 cups heavy cream

2 tablespoons freshly squeezed lemon juice

WINTER BABY BEET SALAD
WITH ORANGES, FRISÉE & PISTACHIOS

Beets provide a splash of color in winter dishes. They are harvested before the ground freezes. I prefer to eat beets cold, like in this winter salad, rather than in hot preparations: For me the flavors stand out more distinctly, especially when the beets are paired with something acidic like oranges. The pistachios add great texture to this salad.

SERVES 4

- 6 baby Chioggia beets, tops trimmed (see Notes)
- 6 baby red beets, tops trimmed
- 6 baby gold beets, tops trimmed
- ⅓ cup sugar
- ⅓ cup white wine vinegar
- 3 sprigs fresh thyme
- 6 whole black peppercorns
- 1 teaspoon chile flakes
  Kosher salt
- 1 head frisée, root end trimmed, washed, leaves cut into 2-inch pieces
- 2 navel oranges, cut into segments (see Notes)
- 2 tablespoons sherry vinegar
- 3 tablespoons extra-virgin olive oil

INGREDIENTS CONTINUE

Put the beets in three separate medium saucepans and equally divide the sugar, white wine vinegar, thyme, peppercorns, and chile flakes among the pans. Cover the beets with cold water and season with salt. Bring to a boil, then lower the heat to a gentle simmer and cook until the beets are easy to pierce with a knife, 10 to 12 minutes.

Remove the beets from the liquid and let sit until cool enough to handle. Using a dish towel, carefully wipe the skin off the beets and trim away any of the remaining tops. Split the beets in half from top to bottom.

Put the beets in a large bowl with the frisée and oranges. Toss with the sherry vinegar and oil; season with salt and white pepper. Arrange on a long serving platter and top with the pistachios. Serve at once.

NOTES: Be careful not to cut into the beets when trimming the tops.

Segmenting citrus (or cutting them into supremes) is easy to do and adds a nice finish to a dish. This technique can be used for segmenting most types of citrus. Cut the top and bottom off the orange so that it sits flat on a surface. With a small, sharp knife, trim away the peel and pith, cutting so that you follow the curve of the orange. Do this around the entire orange, removing the peel and pith in strips, until you are left with only the flesh of the fruit. Orange segments

are held together by a thin membrane. Hold the orange over a small bowl and carefully cut each segment by slicing as close to the membrane as possible. The segments should come out easily when cut on either side; place the segments in the bowl. Once all of the segments have been removed, squeeze any remaining juice from the pith into the bowl. Cover the bowl with plastic wrap and refrigerate for up to 2 days.

Freshly ground white pepper

¼ cup pistachios, lightly toasted and roughly chopped

MAINE LOBSTERS

York, Maine
Mark Sewall

Lobsterman Mark Sewall never filled out a resume or a job application. He simply took to the water and made a living. The day after a massive storm blew across Maine during the fall of 1966, the rocky beaches off York were scattered with tattered lobster cages. Ellsworth Sewall, Mark's father and a lifelong lobsterman, looked out over the wreckage despairingly. He pulled Mark, just a tyke of four years old, down from their pickup truck and started the long process of gathering up his traps. Mark, eager to help his father with the work, walked up to a trap, grabbed the edges of the slick, wooden frame and pulled with all his might. Sadly, the trap wouldn't budge. The couple of bricks used to sink the traps to the ocean floor were too much weight for the toddler's tiny frame. Instead of giving up, he walked over to another trap, this one so roughed up it had lost its bricks, and yanked it straight up to the truck. His dad gave him a funny look and said, "Okay, son. That one's yours."

Four-year-old Mark spent the winter repairing his beaten trap and the following summer used it to haul his first catch. What-

ever he caught, he could keep, his dad said, except for one lobster a week, which would cover the cost of his bait. Mark was a lobsterman from that moment on.

A third-generation fisherman, Mark worked through high school on his father's boat until he could afford his own, which he named *Kelpa* for its natural ability to chew up the kelp on the rocks when it got too close to land. Today, thirty years later, Mark's boat is still named *Kelpa*, and there's nowhere he'd rather be than on the water. "You have to want it," he explains. What that means is that even in the depths of a raging snow squall, when the boat can hardly make it back to land, Mark is out on the water. He's watched wood traps being replaced with metal ones and fancy new navigational equipment bring newcomers out on the water. These improvements make his job just the tiniest bit easier.

Today, Mark hauls in lobsters throughout the summer and fall, but it's during the bitter cold of January and February that he's out there trapping Maine shrimp, which run for just six short weeks. For Mark, it's a good way

to keep the money coming in when the lobstering season quiets down. My restaurants buy all the shrimp he catches, except for what he sells on the docks to the locals—the shrimp arrive still alive in the tubs. The shrimp have to be cleaned the same day they are caught, which means the kitchen crews stay late and stand around, usually with beers in hand, until every last shrimp is processed. They might complain but it's become an annual tradition. Mark delivers lobsters, shrimp, and other seafood to the restaurants every week, oftentimes stopping for a plate of fried clams, oyster sliders, and whatever else he can fuel up on before heading back out to brave the cold from the helm of the *Kelpa*.

CREAMY OYSTER STEW

During the construction of our newest restaurant, Row 34, my partner, Garrett Harker, was on site when the foundation was dug. He looked down and found oyster shells in the old floor. More than a hundred years ago, oyster shells were a common construction material in the Boston area. We took this as a good sign that our "everyman" oyster bar was sitting exactly where it should be. Stew is often thought of as a poor man's food with humble beginnings; for this version, I elevate it ever so slightly with fennel and white wine. But what really makes this dish work is its abundance of oysters.

Shuck the oysters as shown on page 232, reserving the meat and ½ cup of the oyster liquor or juice. Refrigerate until needed.

In a medium saucepan, heat the oil over medium-high heat and add the fennel trimmings, shallot, and garlic; cook until they begin to color lightly, 3 to 4 minutes. Add the wine and bring to a boil. Lower the heat and let simmer for 3 minutes; add the cream and bay leaf and continue to simmer until the cream is reduced by almost half, about 18 minutes. Remove from the heat and strain through a fine-mesh sieve, discarding the solids.

When the cream is nearly reduced, melt the butter in a large saucepan over medium heat. Add the diced fennel and the celery and cook until they become translucent, about 6 minutes. Add the strained cream sauce and bring to a boil. Stir in the lemon juice and zest. Add the oysters and oyster liquor and bring the stew just to a simmer. Remove from the heat and stir in the fennel fronds. Let sit for 30 seconds. Season with salt and white pepper.

Lightly toast the bread slices and place one slice in each of the small shallow serving bowls. Spoon the oyster stew over the bread and serve.

SERVES 4

- 16 medium oysters
- 2 tablespoons canola oil
- 1 small bulb fennel, finely diced, trimmings reserved
- 1 shallot, diced
- 1 garlic clove, minced
- ¼ cup white wine
- 2 cups heavy cream
- 1 bay leaf
- 2 tablespoons unsalted butter
- 1 stalk celery, thinly sliced
- 1 tablespoon freshly squeezed lemon juice
- 2 teaspoons grated lemon zest
- 1 tablespoon fennel fronds
- Kosher salt and freshly ground white pepper
- 4 slices Rustic Bread (page 230)

POACHED WINTER FLOUNDER

Winter flounder is also called black back or lemon sole; it's one of the many fish that have a biological as well as a market name. Smaller ones are usually sold as black backs and larger ones as lemon sole. This type of flounder moves to shallower waters in the winter months. If you've ever been on the Atlantic Ocean in February, you will really appreciate what it takes to get this fish to market—it's not easy. A good dose of citrus, like Meyer lemons, brightens up this dish, which can also be made with regular flounder, sole, or halibut.

SERVES 4

- 3 Meyer lemons
- 8 winter flounder fillets, skin removed
- 8 tablespoons unsalted butter
- ¼ cup white wine
- ¼ cup Chicken Stock (page 218)
- 2 sprigs fresh thyme
- 1 bay leaf
- Kosher salt and freshly ground white pepper
- 1 tablespoon parsley leaves

Preheat the oven to 350°F.

Cut 2 of the lemons into segments (see Notes on page 166). Juice the third lemon and set aside.

Check the flounder fillets to ensure that there are no bones. Fold the fillets so that each end is tucked underneath toward the middle; the two ends of the fillet should be touching but not overlapping.

Using 1 tablespoon of the butter, lightly coat a baking dish large enough to hold all of the fillets. Place the fish in the baking dish, leaving a little space between them. Add the wine, stock, lemon juice, thyme, and bay leaf to the dish and season with salt and white pepper. Cover the dish with foil and bake for 12 minutes.

Transfer the fish to a plate and pour most of the liquid from the baking dish into a medium saucepan. Bring to a boil. Whisk in the remaining 7 tablespoons butter into the liquid and lower the heat to low so that it doesn't come back to a boil. Season with salt and white pepper. Drizzle the fillets with the sauce and top with lemon segments. Garnish with parsley leaves.

Serve with Black Rice (page 194) and Crisp Shallots (page 227).

PAN-ROASTED HAKE

A member of the cod family, hake has long taken a back seat to the more popular cod. But, because so much pressure has been put on other New England fish species, alternatives like hake are becoming popular. This is a simple preparation, but because the butter and lemon enrich the sauce, it's satisfying during the cold, winter months.

Preheat the oven to 375°F.

In a large, oven-safe sauté pan, heat the oil over medium-high heat. Place the hake in the hot oil, presentation side down. Cook for 2 minutes, then lower the heat. Add the butter to the pan and let it brown around the fish for 3 to 4 minutes. Remove the pan from the heat and carefully flip the fish over. Transfer the sauté pan to the oven and bake for 5 minutes.

Remove the fish fillets to a serving platter. Brush the fillets with the lemon juice and garnish with thyme leaves. Season with salt and white pepper.

Serve with Hubbard Squash Puree (page 103) and Vegetable Hash (page 147).

SERVES 4

¼ cup canola oil

4 (7-ounce) hake fillets, skin removed

1 tablespoon unsalted butter

3 tablespoons freshly squeezed lemon juice

1 teaspoon fresh thyme leaves

Kosher salt and freshly ground white pepper

BAKED STUFFED LOBSTER

This recipe is my "fancy" version of a traditional baked, stuffed lobster. I hate the idea of hiding lobster meat with breading. This preparation is just as decadent as the classic rendition but doesn't overwhelm the lobster itself. The winter vegetables—other winter vegetables, such as turnips or rutabagas, can be substituted—and the floral notes of the tarragon complement the other ingredients in this dish. Choose big lobsters and take extra care to get all of the meat out of the shells so that they look beautiful on the plate.

SERVES 4

FOR THE LOBSTERS

4 (1½-pound) hard-shell lobsters

FOR THE STUFFING

12 tablespoons unsalted butter

¼ cup finely diced onion

¼ cup finely diced celery

¼ cup peeled and finely diced carrot

4 cups diced bread, preferably brioche

2 large eggs

2 tablespoons fresh tarragon leaves

1 cup Vegetable Stock (page 220)

Kosher salt and freshly ground black pepper

INGREDIENTS CONTINUE

Prepare the lobster: Steam the lobster (see page 239). Let the lobsters cool in ice water for 10 minutes. Carefully remove the claw meat from the shell, keeping the claw meat intact. Remove the tail from the body and split it in half lengthwise, keeping the meat in the shell. Keep the lobster cold until ready to serve.

Make the stuffing: Preheat the oven to 350°F. Grease an 8-inch-square baking dish with 1 tablespoon of the butter.

In a large sauté pan, melt 8 tablespoons of the butter over medium heat. Add the onion, celery, and carrot and sweat until they begin to soften but are not cooked through or browned, about 5 minutes.

Put the vegetables and any excess butter from the pan in a large bowl; add the bread to the bowl. Stir in the eggs, tarragon, and enough stock to make the stuffing moist but not soggy. Season the stuffing with salt and pepper.

Transfer the stuffing into the prepared baking dish. Dice the remaining 3 tablespoons of butter and dot the top of the stuffing. Bake uncovered for 30 minutes. The top should be golden brown.

RECIPE CONTINUES

RECIPE CONTINUED

FOR THE BUTTER SAUCE & VEGETABLES

¼ cup white wine

¼ cup champagne vinegar

1 shallot, thinly sliced

2 whole black peppercorns

1 bay leaf

2 sprigs fresh thyme

2 cups (2 sticks) cold unsalted butter, cut into 1-inch cubes

Kosher salt and freshly ground black pepper

¼ cup Vegetable Stock (page 220)

Make the butter sauce and vegetables: In a small saucepan, combine the wine, vinegar, shallot, peppercorns, bay leaf, and thyme and bring to a boil; cook until the liquid is reduced to about 2 tablespoons, about 5 minutes. Strain through a fine-mesh sieve and return the liquid to the saucepan, discarding the solids. Over very low heat, whisk in the butter a few cubes at a time, whisking constantly as it melts. The butter sauce should never boil; it should be thick enough to coat a spoon. Season with salt and pepper. Cover and keep warm until ready to use.

Lower the oven temperature to 300°F. Using a round cookie cutter, cut four 4-inch rounds out of the stuffing from the baking dish. Place the rounds on a baking sheet and bake until warmed through.

While the stuffing is warming, put all of the lobster claw and tail meat in another baking dish that is large enough to hold the meat without overlapping the pieces. Pour ½ cup of the butter sauce and the stock over the lobster; it should be almost completely submerged. Place the dish in the oven with the stuffing. Continue heating the stuffing and the lobster for 10 to 15 minutes, until warmed all the way through.

Remove the stuffing and lobster from the oven. Place the stuffing in the center of a serving platter. Carefully place one whole lobster (two tail halves, two claws) on top of the stuffing, interlocking the two pieces of tail and placing the claws on top. Drizzle the remaining sauce over the lobster.

Serve with Rosemary Carrots (page 191) and Cauliflower with Brown Butter and Thyme (page 146).

ROASTED CHICKEN

Everyone needs one good roast chicken recipe in their repertoire—you'll make this one over and over again. I brine my chickens before roasting them, which keeps them moist and infuses flavor throughout the whole bird.

Truss the chickens: Trim the first two small joints off the chicken wings, saving them for a sauce or a stock. Keep the chicken cavity facing you, breast side up; lay a 2-foot piece of butcher's twine under the protruding tail of the chicken. Pull the twine up around the end of the legs, cross over, and pull tight. You should end up with the legs and the tail pulled together. Pull the twine between the breast and the thighs. Loop the twine around the back of the thighs on both sides and turn the chicken over. Cross the twine over the chicken wings so that they lay flat against the bird. Tie the twine into a firm knot.

Place the trussed chickens in a container large enough to hold them both and add the brine. Let sit at room temperature, covered, for 2 hours.

Preheat the oven to 400°F.

Remove the chickens from the brine and pat dry. Place them in a roasting pan large enough to hold both birds.

In a small saucepan, melt the butter over medium heat with the garlic, thyme, and sage. Liberally brush the outside of the chickens with the butter, reserving about 2 tablespoons for later use. Season the outsides with salt and pepper. Roast for 10 minutes. Lower the oven temperature to 300°F and roast for 1 hour. Remove from the oven and let sit for at least 20 minutes.

With a sharp knife, cut the chicken meat away from the bone, starting at the breast and moving the knife down toward the leg and thigh; each half-chicken should have the leg and thigh bones as well as the wing bone still connected to the breast.

Lay the chickens on a baking sheet, skin side up. Brush with the remaining herb butter and put back in the oven for 10 minutes. Remove and serve with the Chicken Sauce on the side.

RECIPE CONTINUES

SERVES 4

- 2 (3-pound) whole chickens, giblets removed
- 1 recipe (about 1 gallon) Brine (page 221)
- ½ cup (1 stick) unsalted butter
- 2 garlic cloves, crushed
- 3 sprigs fresh thyme
- 3 fresh sage leaves
- Kosher salt and freshly ground black pepper
- ¾ cup Chicken Sauce (recipe follows)

CHICKEN SAUCE

MAKES ABOUT 1 CUP

In a large saucepan, heat the oil over medium-high heat; add the shallots and cook until they begin to brown, about 3 minutes, stirring frequently. Add the garlic and cook until it is just starting to color, about 1 minute or so.

Remove from the heat and pour off any excess oil from the pan. Add the wine and simmer until reduced by half; add the stock, peppercorns, and thyme. Let the sauce simmer gently until there is a little more than 1 cup of liquid left in the pan, about 30 minutes. Strain the sauce through a fine-mesh sieve, discarding the solids, and refrigerate in an airtight container until ready to use or up to 4 days.

Just before using the sauce, bring it to a simmer. Add the vinegar and whisk in the butter. Do not boil after the butter has been added; season with salt and serve.

Serve with Rosemary Carrots (page 191) and Scallion Whipped Potatoes (page 225).

- 3 tablespoons canola oil
- 2 shallots, thinly sliced
- 1 garlic clove, crushed
- 1 cup white wine
- 4 cups Dark Chicken Stock (page 219)
- 3 whole black peppercorns
- 2 sprigs fresh thyme
- 1 teaspoon sherry vinegar
- 2 tablespoons unsalted butter
- Kosher salt

UPDATED YANKEE POT ROAST

This classic New England dish has humble beginnings. It's made its way through many generations of family kitchens and has changed little from the original recipe. I use veal stock to give it more richness, and reduce the braising liquid to amp up the final presentation. Some butchers will have chuck rolls ready to cook, but you might have to order one from your butcher a few days before preparing this roast. Request one that's uniform in size so that it cooks evenly.

SERVES 6

¼ cup canola oil

1 (5-pound) chuck roll

Kosher salt and freshly ground black pepper

1 large carrot, peeled and cut into 1-inch pieces

1 large Spanish onion, cut into 1-inch pieces

2 celery stalks, cut into 1-inch pieces

2 quarts Veal Stock (page 220)

2 cups red wine

3 sprigs fresh thyme

2 bay leaves

1 small head garlic, cut in half

1 small leek, split lengthwise and washed

Preheat the oven to 300°F.

In a sauté pan that's large enough to comfortably hold the chuck roll, heat the oil over high heat. Season the chuck well with salt and pepper and sear on all sides until the exterior is a deep brown color, about 3 minutes per side. (You should not turn the roll until it releases easily from the pan.) Once all the sides are seared, remove the chuck roll to a plate and turn the heat down to medium-high. Add the carrot, onion, and celery and cook, stirring frequently, until they are lightly browned, 4 to 5 minutes. Remove from the heat.

Transfer the seared chuck roll and vegetables to a large oven-safe braising pot that has a lid. Pour the stock and wine into the braising pot; there should be enough liquid to almost cover the meat. Put the thyme, bay leaves, garlic halves, and leek into the pot and slowly bring to a boil, uncovered. Cover and transfer the pot to the oven. Bake for about 3½ hours. Remove the pan and test the roast by piercing with a paring knife or roasting fork. The meat should be tender but not falling apart. Let cool in the liquid for 20 minutes. Reserve a few tablespoons of the braising liquid. Remove the meat to a cutting board to rest.

Strain the remaining braising liquid through a fine-mesh sieve into a saucepan, discarding the vegetables; you should

have about 3 cups liquid. Simmer the strained liquid over medium heat until reduced by half, about 15 minutes. Keep warm until ready to serve.

Remove the string from the roast. Carve the meat into 6 slices and place on a serving platter. Keep the meat moist by drizzling a little of the braising liquid over the slices. Serve with the reduced sauce on the side.

ROASTED DUCK LEG CONFIT

Just like salt cod, confiting duck meat came about as a way to preserve protein when there was no refrigeration. Traditionally, the duck is salted and then cooked in its own fat. Like many techniques, the process has evolved—but not too much, especially since anything that is cooked in its own fat tastes delicious. Duck and duck fat are now available in specialty markets and through a number of online purveyors. (See Resources page 244).

Put the ¼ cup salt, peppercorns, thyme, rosemary, and bay leaves in a food processor and pulse until thoroughly combined. Sprinkle the mixture lightly over the skin of the duck legs, coating it evenly.

Place the duck legs in an airtight container and refrigerate for up to 8 hours. Remove the duck legs from the refrigerator and rinse off the salt mixture; pat dry.

Preheat the oven to 250°F.

In a saucepan, warm the duck fat over medium-low heat until it liquefies.

Put the duck legs in a large, oven-safe braising pot that will fit all of them snugly and pour the duck fat over the top so that the legs are covered. Bake for 4 to 6 hours; the duck should be very tender but not falling apart.

Remove the pot from the oven and let the duck legs cool in the fat. When they are cool enough to handle, carefully remove the thigh bones, making sure to keep the legs intact. (The duck may be prepared to this point 1 to 2 days ahead. Place in an airtight container and refrigerate until ready to serve.)

Preheat the broiler and position a rack in the middle of the oven. Place the duck legs on a baking sheet and broil to brown them. Move the legs frequently so that they brown evenly and are warmed through. Serve the legs whole.

Serve with Toasted Barley with Chantenay Carrots and Pomegranate (page 195).

SERVES 4

¼ cup kosher salt, plus more to taste

6 whole black peppercorns

2 sprigs fresh thyme

1 sprig fresh rosemary

2 bay leaves

4 duck legs, extra skin trimmed off

3 cups duck fat

SIMPLE SAUSAGE & BEANS

Sausage is so simple to make—and this recipe is a great place to start. Prepare the sausage a day in advance and let it sit in the refrigerator so that the flavors of the spices deepen. The beans taste even better a day after they've been cooked. I like to use dried white beans for this dish, but there are so many varieties out there today, it's well worth experimenting.

SERVES 6

FOR THE SAUSAGE

2 tablespoons fennel seeds

1 tablespoon whole black peppercorns

2 teaspoons curry powder

2 teaspoons chile flakes

1 tablespoon kosher salt

2 tablespoons canola oil

1 small Spanish onion, minced

2 garlic cloves, minced

2 pounds ground pork

Make the sausage: Grind the fennel and peppercorns in a spice grinder or small blender. In a small bowl, combine the fennel and peppercorns with the curry powder, chile flakes, and salt; set aside.

Heat 1 tablespoon of the oil in a sauté pan over medium heat, add the onion and garlic, and cook until they become translucent but not browned, about 4 minutes. Remove from the pan and let cool completely in the refrigerator.

Put the pork and the spice mixture in the bowl of a food processor (you may have to do this in two batches). Pulse until thoroughly combined and the pork is somewhat smooth. Transfer to a large bowl and fold in the chilled onion and garlic.

Place an 18 by 12–inch piece of plastic wrap on a flat surface. Layer the sheet with two more pieces of the same size. Position the layered sheets so a long end is closest to you.

Place one quarter of the pork mixture in a line across the plastic, leaving 2 inches of plastic on each end and 2 inches from the edge closest to you. Roll the plastic over the pork and fold it under the meat, tucking the edge of the wrap tightly underneath the meat. Roll the plastic wrap into a cylinder, pinching the ends to force the pork toward the center of the cylinder. Twist each end of the plastic wrap in opposite directions to force the pork into a cylinder shape. When it is very firm, tie off each end with kitchen twine. Smooth down the exposed edge

RECIPE CONTINUES

FOR THE BEANS

3 cups dried white beans

1 bunch red Swiss chard

3 tablespoons canola oil

3 garlic cloves, minced

1 small Spanish onion, minced

2 tablespoons tomato paste

8 cups Chicken Stock (page 219) or Vegetable Stock (page 220)

Kosher salt and freshly ground black pepper

1 tablespoon sherry vinegar

RECIPE CONTINUED

of the plastic wrap along the length of the sausage. The plastic wrap should not have any holes or tears in it and no pork should be coming out of either end. Refrigerate the pork cylinders for up to 24 hours. Repeat this process with the remaining pork. You will end up with 4 large sausages.

Make the beans: Rinse the beans and soak them in a large bowl of cold water for 1 hour.

Pour off the water and place the soaked beans in a large pot with fresh cold water. Bring to a boil and cook for 1 minute. Drain the beans.

Remove the leaves from the stems of the chard. Thinly slice the stems and reserve the leaves. Set aside.

Heat 1 tablespoon of the oil in a large saucepot over medium-high heat. Add the garlic, onion, and chard stems; cook, stirring frequently, until the vegetables begin to color lightly, 3 to 4 minutes. Add the tomato paste and stir to coat the vegetables until they take on a slightly darker color, about 1 minute. Stir in the beans and stock. Season with salt and let simmer until the beans are tender but not mushy, 30 to 40 minutes.

Transfer about one quarter of the beans with some of the cooking liquid to a food processor and puree until smooth. Fold the pureed beans back into the remaining beans; season with salt, pepper, and vinegar. Just before serving, fold in the chard leaves.

Preheat the oven to 325°F.

In a pot large enough to hold all of the sausages, bring water to a boil. Add the sausages and simmer for 7 minutes.

Carefully remove the sausages and let rest until cool enough to handle. Use a sharp knife to remove the plastic wrap, being careful not to pierce the sausages.

Heat the remaining oil in a sauté pan over medium-high heat and sear the sausages on all sides.

Put the sausages on a baking sheet and bake for 4 minutes. Slice the sausages into 2-inch pieces. Spoon the beans onto a large platter, top with the sliced sausage meat, and serve.

BRAISED PORK SHANKS

Pork shanks are delicious when they're braised. Ask your butcher for a horizontal cut on the shank, or an osso bucco cut; they cook a little quicker but look awesome on the plate. Order the shanks a few days in advance, since it takes time for the butcher to prepare them; if you can't find cut ones, whole shanks can be used.

Preheat the oven to 300°F.

In a large sauté pan, heat the oil over medium-high heat. Season the pork shanks all over with salt and pepper and sear in the oil on both sides until they're golden brown and release easily from the pan, about 3 minutes per side.

Remove the shanks from the pan and place them in an oven-safe braising pot that's deep enough to allow them to be submerged in liquid.

To the oil remaining in the sauté pan, add the onion, celery, and carrots and cook over medium-high heat until lightly browned, about 5 minutes. Drain any excess fat from the pan. Transfer the vegetables to the braising pot with the shanks.

To the sauté pan, add the wine and bring to a boil. Add as much of the stock to the sauté pan as will fit and return to a boil. Pour the boiling liquid over the shanks.

Bring the rest of the stock to a boil in the sauté pan and add that to the shanks along with the bay leaves, thyme, rosemary, and garlic. The shanks should fit snugly in the braising pot and be completely covered with liquid.

Place the braising pot in the oven and cook for 1½ hours. The shanks should be almost falling off the bone and easy to penetrate with a paring knife. Remove from the oven and let the shanks cool in the liquid for 30 minutes.

Pour 3 cups of the braising liquid into a saucepan and bring to a low simmer; simmer gently until the liquid is reduced to

RECIPE CONTINUES

SERVES 4

- ½ cup canola oil
- 8 pieces pork shank, cut osso bucco style (6 to 8 ounces each)
- Kosher salt and freshly ground black pepper
- 1 cup diced onion
- ½ cup diced celery
- ½ cup diced carrots
- 2 cups red wine
- 3 quarts Chicken Stock (page 219)
- 2 bay leaves
- 4 sprigs fresh thyme
- 2 sprigs fresh rosemary
- 2 garlic cloves

about 1 cup, about 25 minutes. Strain the liquid through a fine-mesh sieve, discarding the solids, and keep warm.

Return the braising pot with the shanks and remaining braising liquid to the oven and lower the oven temperature to 200°F; heat until warmed through. To serve, place two shanks in each of four serving bowls; spoon the warm, reduced braising liquid over the shanks and serve.

Serve with Savoy Cabbage with Red Potatoes and Rutabaga (page 192).

ROSEMARY CARROTS

These carrots are a great way to add color to a winter meal—and, due to the rosemary, they make for a tasty side dish.

Put the carrots in a medium saucepan and cover with water. Season well with salt and bring to a simmer over medium-high heat. Cook until the carrots are tender but not quite cooked through. With a slotted spoon, remove the carrots from the water and let cool.

In a large sauté pan, melt the butter over medium heat and add the rosemary. Cook for about 20 seconds, making sure the butter does not color. Add the carrots and stir to coat evenly with the butter. Sauté until the carrots are warmed through; season with salt and pepper and serve hot.

SERVES 4

20 baby carrots, 4 to 5 inches long, peeled, tops trimmed

Kosher salt

¼ cup unsalted butter

1 tablespoon very finely chopped rosemary

Freshly ground black pepper

SAVOY CABBAGE
WITH RED POTATOES & RUTABAGA

Savoy is a wonderful cabbage that has a robust flavor. This recipe calls for basic root vegetables that, when combined, create a hearty, soulful addition to a winter meal.

SERVES 4

2 rutabagas

8 tablespoons unsalted butter

1 tablespoon kosher salt, plus more to taste

1 pound red potatoes, washed and cut into quarters

Freshly ground black pepper

1 small head savoy cabbage

1 tablespoon finely chopped fresh flat-leaf parsley

Preheat the oven to 350°F.

Peel the rutabagas and cut them into 1-inch cubes. Put in a medium saucepan and cover with water. Add 2 tablespoons of the butter and 1 tablespoon salt. Bring to a simmer over medium-high heat and cook until the rutabagas are tender but not cooked through, about 10 minutes. Remove from the heat and let cool in the cooking liquid for 15 minutes. Drain.

In a large oven-safe sauté pan, heat 4 tablespoons of the butter over medium heat and add the potatoes in a single layer, cut side down; season with salt and pepper. Cook for 4 to 5 minutes, then remove from the heat as soon as the butter begins to color. Transfer the sauté pan of potatoes to the oven; roast for 20 minutes, or until the potatoes are cooked through. Remove from the oven and let cool.

Cut the base off the cabbage so that the leaves separate. Cut the core out of each leaf by making a V-shape cut; cut the leaves into 1- to 2-inch pieces.

In a large sauté pan, melt the remaining 2 tablespoons butter over medium-high heat and add the cabbage, potatoes, and rutabaga. Season with salt and pepper and cook until the cabbage begins to wilt slightly. Toss in the parsley and serve at once.

MACOMBER TURNIP GRATIN

According to legend, Aiden and Elihu Macomber planted this turnip (a type of rutabaga) in Westport, Massachusetts, in 1876. Prized for being snow white on the inside and especially flavorful, it remains a popular local ingredient, and even has its own plaque at the entrance of the town. It's now grown all over New England and beyond—but Westport holds firmly to its bragging rights. To honor the vegetable, I like to layer it with potatoes and cream in a rich and hearty gratin. If you can't find Macomber turnips, just about any turnip or rutabaga will do.

In a small saucepan, combine the cream, garlic, and nutmeg; bring to a boil, then remove from the heat and let sit, covered, at room temperature until ready to use.

Preheat the oven to 350°F.

Using half of the butter, generously grease a 10-inch-square baking dish.

Peel the turnips and potatoes. Using a mandolin or a very sharp knife, carefully cut the turnips and potatoes into ⅛-inch slices. Starting with the potato, shingle the pieces together to create a layer on the bottom of the baking dish, then add a layer of turnips; alternate, making sure that the top layer is turnip and seasoning every other layer with salt and pepper as you build the gratin.

Remove the garlic from the cream and pour the cream mixture over the potato and turnip; it should come up to just below the top layer. Dot the remaining butter over the top of the gratin and bake for 25 to 30 minutes, until the vegetables are tender all the way through and the top is golden brown. Let stand for a few minutes before serving. Serve hot.

(See image on page 153).

SERVES 4 TO 6

- 3 cups heavy cream
- 2 garlic cloves, crushed
- ½ teaspoon freshly grated nutmeg
- 2 large Macomber turnips
- 2 large Yukon gold potatoes
- ½ cup (1 stick) unsalted butter, softened
- Kosher salt and freshly ground black pepper

BLACK RICE

There is nothing particularly "New England" about black rice, but I like the way it complements most fish. It's also a nice change of pace in the winter. There are different varieties of black rice, and so cooking times may vary; taste the rice as you go to make sure you're not overcooking it.

SERVES 4 TO 6

1 tablespoon canola oil (plus 1 more tablespoon if reheating)

¼ cup minced Spanish onion

1 cup black rice

2 cups Vegetable Stock (page 220)

1 bay leaf

Kosher salt

In a medium saucepan with a lid, heat the oil over medium heat, add the onion, and sweat until it's translucent, about 4 minutes. Stir in the rice, add the stock and bay leaf, and season with salt; bring to a simmer and cook, covered, until the rice is tender but still has nice texture, about 30 minutes. (The cooking time may vary depending on the variety of black rice you use.)

Drain off any excess liquid; cover and keep warm if using immediately or spread on a baking sheet and let cool. The rice may be prepared up to 3 days ahead and refrigerated in an airtight container. To reheat, heat rice in a medium saucepan over low heat until warmed through. Add 1 tablespoon canola oil to help break up the rice.

TOASTED BARLEY
WITH CHANTENAY CARROTS & POMEGRANATE

Chantenay carrots are an heirloom variety from the Chantenay region of France. They were first cultivated in the eighteenth century and are a hardy breed that does well in cool growing climates. They have an amazing earthy, sweet taste. I add them to toasted pearl barley for a filling side dish. The pomegranate brightens all of the flavors and pairs especially well with these carrots.

In a medium saucepan, heat the oil over medium heat. Add the garlic and shallot and cook until translucent, about 2 to 3 minutes. Stir in the barley and cook until lightly toasted, about 5 minutes. Add the stock and bring to a boil. Lower the heat to a simmer and season with salt and pepper. Let simmer for about 20 minutes; the barley should be tender but not mushy. Pour any excess liquid into a small bowl and set the liquid aside. Spread the barley on a baking sheet until ready to use.

In a medium saucepan, cover the carrots with cold water and add the butter; season well with salt. Bring to a simmer over medium-high heat and cook until the carrots are tender but not cooked all the way through, about 8 minutes. Drain and let cool.

In a large sauté pan, combine the carrots and barley along with 3 tablespoons of the barley cooking liquid. Cook over medium heat until the barley and carrots are warm, 3 to 4 minutes. Toss in the chives and pomegranate seeds and season with salt and pepper. Serve warm.

SERVES 4

2 tablespoons canola oil

1 garlic clove, minced

1 large shallot, minced

1 cup pearl barley

2 cups Chicken Stock (page 219)

Kosher salt and freshly ground black pepper

2 large Chantenay carrots, peeled and diced (about ¾ cup)

2 tablespoons unsalted butter

1 tablespoon minced fresh chives

½ cup pomegranate seeds

SEASONAL DESSERTS

There is a strong New England tradition when it comes to making desserts. This region is the birthplace of the Boston cream pie, cobblers, and the whoopie pie. But like most of the cuisine of this region, those dishes are continually being updated, in kitchens including my own, to create "new" classics.

Dessert has a way of lifting everyone's spirits, particularly seasonal favorites like pumpkin pie for Thanksgiving and summer berry shortcake for the Fourth of July. Make the most of each season's offerings.

My wife, Lisa, is the dessert master in our home. I met Lisa years ago when we were both working at L'Espalier in Boston. She was the pastry chef and created extraordinary desserts. Meanwhile, I prefer savory cooking and enjoy eating desserts more than I enjoy making them—just one of the reasons why Lisa and I make such a great team.

Luckily, she's shared with me some of her professional know-how along the way, and I've developed some tasty desserts that are so easy to make even I enjoy preparing them.

Don't stress about dessert. It's one of the few parts of a meal that can usually be made ahead of time. Keep extra dough or biscuits on hand in the freezer, and you'll have the makings of a sweet ending whenever you need it. And, like anything, good desserts take practice. Try these recipes a few times and you'll understand how enjoyable it can be to make a fine dessert.

SEASONAL DESSERTS

CHERRY COBBLER

Cobblers were originally invented by British settlers, who found they were unable to re-create their native dessert, suet pudding, due to a lack of the proper ingredients. Like any good New Englander, though, they used what they had on hand, and the tradition eventually grew to include a range of delightfully named siblings including the slump, the dump, and the Betty. Serve my version of a traditional cobbler with vanilla bean ice cream and make sure to eat it while the fruit filling is still warm.

Preheat the oven to 375°F. Lightly grease an 8-inch pie dish with butter.

Make the filling: In a large saucepan, combine the cherries, sugar, salt, ¼ cup water, and the cornstarch; place over medium heat. Cook until the mixture is bubbling and thickened, about 5 minutes. Pour the mixture into the prepared pie dish.

Make the topping: In a medium bowl, combine the flour, sugar, cinnamon, nutmeg, ginger, baking powder, and salt. Cut the butter into ¼-inch pieces and work into the flour mixture with a pastry cutter or your fingers until the mixture appears sandy and begins to hold together.

In a small bowl, mix together the egg and milk, then add to the flour mixture. Mix until the batter is just combined.

Drop tablespoons of the batter over the cherries and bake for 12 to 15 minutes, until the top of the cobbler is golden brown and the fruit is bubbling. Serve warm or at room temperature.

SERVES 6 TO 8

FOR THE FILLING

8 cups fresh cherries, pitted

1 cup sugar

¼ teaspoon kosher salt

1 tablespoon cornstarch

FOR THE TOPPING

1 cup all-purpose flour

⅓ cup granulated sugar

½ teaspoon ground cinnamon

¼ teaspoon freshly grated nutmeg

¼ teaspoon ground ginger

1 teaspoon baking powder

¼ teaspoon kosher salt

4 tablespoons (½ stick) unsalted butter, plus more for the pie dish

1 large egg

3 tablespoons whole milk

LEMON TART
WITH LAVENDER CREAM

This delicious dessert combines the ethereal smoothness of lemon curd with the fragrant aroma of lavender in the accompanying cream. It's also simple to make. You should prepare the curd a day ahead of time to give it time to cool and set up; the tart crust can be made in advance, too.

SERVES 8

- 1 tablespoon unsalted butter
- 1 recipe Pastry Dough (see page 229)
- 9 large egg yolks
- 3 large whole eggs
- 1 cup granulated sugar
- 1 cup freshly squeezed lemon juice
- 1 cup heavy cream
- 1 tablespoon dried lavender flowers
- 3 tablespoons confectioners' sugar

Preheat the oven to 375°F. Lightly grease a 9-inch fluted tart pan with the butter.

On a lightly floured surface, roll out the dough to a round about ¼ inch thick. Place the prepared tart pan on top of the dough to measure, then cut out a circle that is about 1½ inches larger than the pan. Fold the circle of dough in half, transfer to the pan, and unfold. Fit the dough into the corners and ridges of the pan. There will be some dough hanging over—leave it for now.

Place the tart shell in the refrigerator for 20 minutes. Remove it from the refrigerator and cut away any excess overhang by pressing the dough off with your finger at the edge of the pan.

Lay a piece of parchment over the tart dough and fill with dried beans or pie weights. Bake the dough for about 15 minutes. The crust should be golden brown. Remove from the oven, remove the pie weights, and let the crust cool completely.

In a medium stainless-steel bowl, use a whisk to combine the egg yolks, whole eggs, and granulated sugar thoroughly. Whisk in the lemon juice.

Heat 2 to 3 cups water in a small saucepan until simmering. Place the bowl with the egg mixture over the saucepan and stir constantly with a rubber spatula, making sure to scrape along the entire bottom and sides of the bowl. When the mixture begins to thicken, after about 4 minutes, whisk vigorously, 2 to 3 minutes. The mixture should coat your whisk and be the consistency of pudding.

Remove the bowl of lemon curd from the heat and immediately pour it through a fine-mesh sieve into a storage container.

Cover the top with plastic wrap so it touches the surface of the curd. Refrigerate until cool or overnight.

Heat ¼ cup of the cream in a small saucepan over medium heat. Add the lavender. When the cream starts to bubble around the edges, remove it from the heat and let steep, uncovered, at room temperature for 20 minutes. Pour the cream through a fine-mesh sieve and discard the lavender. Stir in the remaining ¾ cup cream and confectioners' sugar and whisk until it begins to form soft peaks.

Transfer the chilled curd to a bowl and whisk until smooth. Pour the curd into the tart shell and smooth the top with a rubber spatula. Chill for 1 hour in the refrigerator. Serve the tart with the lavender cream on the side.

SUMMER BERRIES
WITH WHIPPED CREAM & BUTTERMILK BISCUITS

This dish is my New England take on the classic shortcake. I use a biscuit to stack the cream and seasonal fruit, offering a simple way to showcase both. The key to a great biscuit is in the way you mix the dough; don't overmix it or the biscuits will be tough.

Make the biscuits: In a large bowl, combine the flour, salt, sugar, and baking powder.

Grate the butter on the large holes of a box grater. With a rubber spatula, gently fold the butter into the flour mixture until the flour appears mealy but there are still large, pea-size pieces of butter. Make a well in the center of the flour mixture and pour in the buttermilk. Fold gently with a rubber spatula until the dough just comes together. The texture will be very shaggy and crumbly.

Transfer the dough to a lightly floured surface, and pat it together into a rectangle. Roll the dough into a roughly 12 by 16–inch rectangle, then fold it into thirds. Roll the dough out again, and repeat the folding and rolling 2 or 3 times. Finally, roll it out to 1 inch thick and cut into 3-inch-square biscuits.

Preheat the oven to 350°F. Line a baking sheet with parchment paper.

Place the biscuit squares in an airtight container and freeze for 20 minutes.

Place the frozen biscuit squares on the prepared baking sheet. Bake for 10 to 12 minutes, until the biscuits are golden brown. Let cool completely on wire racks, then split each in half horizontally. Place the bottom halves on individual serving dishes.

Make the cream and berries: In a small bowl, combine the berries, then spoon about ¼ cup over each of the halved biscuits. Place a dollop of whipped cream over the berries. Place the top halves of the biscuits off-center to show off the berries. Serve immediately.

SERVES 6

FOR THE BISCUITS

6½ cups all-purpose flour, plus more for the work surface

2 tablespoons kosher salt

¼ cup granulated sugar

⅓ cup baking powder

1½ cups (3 sticks) plus 2 tablespoons cold unsalted butter

2⅔ cups buttermilk

FOR THE CREAM AND BERRIES

1 cup fresh raspberries

1 cup fresh blackberries

1 cup small, fresh strawberries, hulled and halved

Whipped cream (see page 215)

SUMMER MELONS
WITH HONEYCOMB & PEPPERED CRÈME FRAÎCHE

When melons are at their peak, it's time to make this perfect end-of-summer dessert. I use cantaloupe and watermelon, but choose from whatever melons you find at the market. The heat from the black pepper adds a bite to this dessert. Look for honeycomb at farmers' markets in the summer or at specialty stores.

SERVES 4 TO 6

- 1 small ripe cantaloupe
- 1 small yellow seedless watermelon
- Pinch of kosher salt
- 1 cup crème fraîche
- 1 teaspoon freshly ground black pepper
- 1 (4 by 4–inch) piece of honeycomb

Rinse the melons and cut off the ends so they stand flat on a cutting board. Using a sharp knife, carefully cut away the melon rinds by slicing from top to bottom, following the curve of the melon and turning after each cut. Cut the cantaloupe in half down the center and remove the seeds. Cut both melons into 2-inch chunks and place them in a large, shallow serving bowl. Sprinkle the melon chunks with the salt.

In a small bowl, combine the crème fraîche and pepper, then place a dollop in the center of the melons. Serve the honeycomb on the side on its own plate with a butter knife. To eat, spread a small piece of honeycomb and crème fraîche on each bite of melon.

FREE-FORM BLUEBERRY TART

I like this dessert because it has all the qualities of a pie but appears a little more rustic. A good fruit pie is all about the ripeness and quality of the main ingredient—blueberries always taste better if you pick them yourself (or at least purchase them from the farmers' market).

SERVES 4 TO 6

1 recipe Pastry Dough (page 229)

¼ cup sugar, plus more for sprinkling

2 teaspoons finely grated lemon zest

¼ cup all-purpose flour

4 cups blueberries

2 tablespoons freshly squeezed lemon juice

1 large egg white, beaten

Line a large baking sheet with parchment paper. Unwrap the dough and place it on a lightly floured surface. Roll out to a 14-inch round about ⅛ inch thick. Fold the dough in half and transfer it to the prepared baking sheet. Unfold the dough and refrigerate for 15 minutes.

Preheat the oven to 375°F.

Make the filling: In a large bowl, combine the sugar, lemon zest, and flour. Fold in the blueberries and lemon juice and let stand for 15 minutes.

Remove the pastry dough round from the refrigerator. Leaving the dough on the prepared baking sheet, spoon the blueberry mixture into the center of the round, leaving a 1½-inch border all around. Fold the dough border up and over the blueberries, pleating it as necessary. Brush the outside of the tart with the egg white and sprinkle with sugar. Bake for about 55 minutes, until the pastry is golden brown and the filling starts to bubble.

Transfer the baking sheet to a rack and let the tart cool slightly. Cut into wedges and serve warm or at room temperature.

NOTE: To make individual tarts, as shown, divide the dough into four equal pieces. Roll the pieces of dough into balls and flatten with your hand. Roll out the circle to about 6 inches around and ⅛ inch thick, then spoon equal portions of the filling into the center of each, leaving a 1½-inch border. Fold and prepare tarts as instructed above. Shorten baking time to 35 to 40 minutes, or until golden brown and bubbling.

PUMPKIN CHIFFON PIE

My version of pumpkin pie is a little lighter then the classic but just as satisfying. Traditionally a Thanksgiving staple, this dessert makes a great addition to any fall meal.

SERVES 8

FOR THE PIE DOUGH

2½ cups all-purpose flour, plus more for the work surface

½ teaspoon kosher salt

1 cup (2 sticks) cold unsalted butter, plus more for the pie dish

6 tablespoons ice water

INGREDIENTS CONTINUE

Preheat the oven to 400°F. Grease an 8-inch pie dish with butter.

Make the pie dough: With a wooden spoon, combine the flour and salt in a large bowl. Cut the butter into ½-inch cubes and add to the flour. Mix together with your hands, or a pastry cutter, until the butter pieces are the size of peas. Add the ice water and stir to incorporate. When the mixture is moist and crumbly, knead it together to form a shaggy dough. The texture will appear a bit dry, but the dough will hydrate as it rests. Wrap the dough in plastic wrap and refrigerate for at least 2 hours.

Unwrap the dough and place it on a lightly floured surface, then sprinkle the top with more flour. Roll out to a round ¼ inch thick. Transfer to the prepared pie dish, then trim and crimp the edges.

Refrigerate the pie shell for 15 minutes, then cover the shell with parchment paper and fill with pie weights or dried beans. Bake until golden brown, 30 to 45 minutes. Remove from the oven, remove the pie weights and paper, and let cool completely.

RECIPE CONTINUES

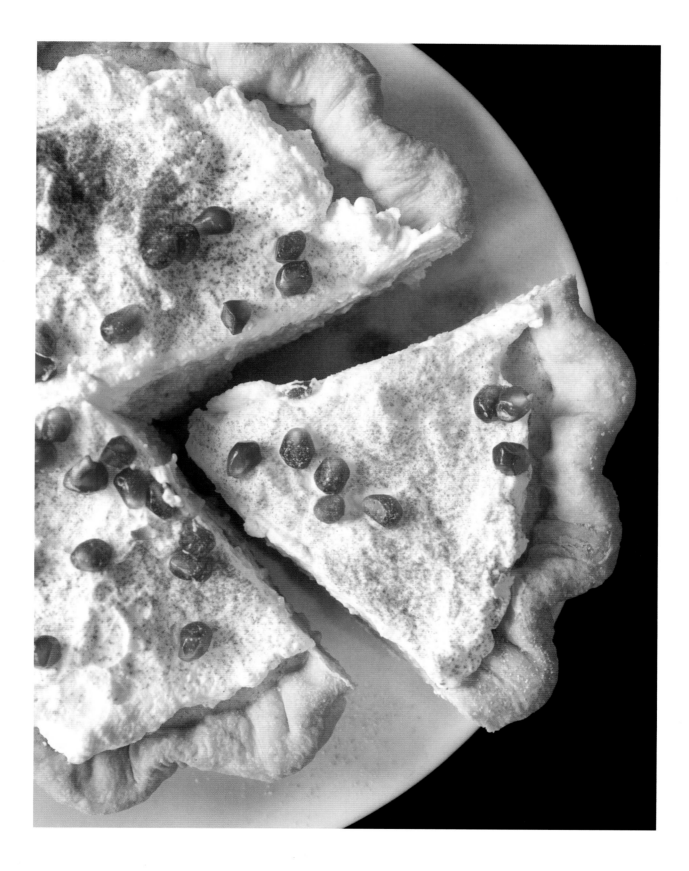

FOR THE FILLING

2¼ teaspoons powdered gelatin

1½ cups canned pumpkin puree

¾ cup sugar

½ teaspoon ground ginger

½ teaspoon ground cinnamon

½ teaspoon ground cloves

¼ teaspoon freshly grated nutmeg

½ teaspoon kosher salt

½ cup whole milk

3 large eggs, separated

¼ teaspoon cream of tartar

Whipped cream (see page 215)

2 tablespoons pomegranate seeds

RECIPE CONTINUED

Make the filling: In a small bowl, sprinkle the powdered gelatin over ¼ cup water. Set aside.

In a medium-size heavy saucepan, combine the pumpkin, ½ cup of the sugar, the ginger, cinnamon, cloves, nutmeg, and salt. Stir constantly over medium heat until the mixture starts to sputter. Reduce the heat to low and continue to cook for 3 to 5 minutes, until thick and shiny. Transfer the mixture to a blender and process for 1 minute. You may need to scrape the mixture down with a spatula to incorporate everything; the pumpkin will be very thick. With the blender running, pour in the milk. Add 1 egg yolk at a time. Add the gelatin mixture and pulse to combine. Return the mixture to the saucepan and stir constantly over medium heat for 3 minutes, or until thickened slightly. Pour the mixture into a bowl and set the bowl in an ice bath to cool, stirring occasionally.

In the bowl of a stand mixer fitted with the whisk attachment, beat the egg whites together with the cream of tartar. When the egg whites form soft peaks, gradually add the remaining ¼ cup sugar, 2 tablespoons at a time. Beat the egg whites until stiff peaks form. Gently fold the egg whites into the cooled pumpkin mixture. Spoon the mixture into the cooled pie shell and chill for at least 2 hours in the refrigerator. Once the pie is cool, top with whipped cream and pomegranate seeds.

APPLE CIDER DOUGHNUTS

Cider doughnuts are a staple at apple orchards throughout New England. Apple-picking season is brief and so, too, is the availability of fresh apple cider. Take advantage of this time to make these flavorful doughnuts at home.

In a small saucepan over medium or medium-low heat, gently simmer the apple cider until it is reduced to about ¼ cup, 20 to 30 minutes. Set aside to cool.

Meanwhile, in a medium bowl, combine the flour, baking powder, baking soda, salt, cinnamon, and nutmeg. Set aside.

Using an electric mixer on medium speed (or in a bowl of a stand mixer fitted with the paddle attachment), beat the butter and sugar together until the mixture is smooth. Add the eggs one at a time and continue to beat until the eggs are completely incorporated. Use a rubber spatula to scrape down the sides of the bowl occasionally. Reduce the speed to low and gradually add the reduced apple cider and the buttermilk, mixing until just combined. At this stage the mixture may look lumpy and uneven. Add the flour mixture and continue to mix until the dough just comes together.

Line two baking sheets with parchment or waxed paper and sprinkle them generously with flour. Turn the dough onto one of the sheets and sprinkle the top with flour. Flatten the dough with your hands until it is about ½ inch thick. Use more flour if the dough is still wet. Transfer the baking sheet with the dough, uncovered, to the freezer until the dough is slightly hardened, about 20 minutes. Take the dough out of the freezer. It should be firm, not frozen.

Using a 3-inch doughnut cutter, cut out doughnut shapes. Place the cut doughnuts and doughnut holes onto the second baking sheet. Refrigerate them for 20 to 30 minutes. (You may

RECIPE CONTINUES

1 cup fresh apple cider

3½ cups all-purpose flour, plus more for dusting

2 teaspoons baking powder

1 teaspoon baking soda

½ teaspoon kosher salt

½ teaspoon ground cinnamon

⅛ teaspoon freshly grated nutmeg

½ cup (1 stick) unsalted butter, at room temperature

1 cup sugar

2 large eggs

½ cup buttermilk

4 cups canola oil

Glaze (recipe follows)

RECIPE CONTINUED

re-roll the scraps of dough, refrigerate briefly, and cut additional doughnuts from the excess dough.)

In a fry-o-later or a heavy-bottom pot, heat the oil until it reaches 350°F on a deep-frying thermometer. Carefully add a few doughnuts to the oil, being sure not to crowd the pan, and fry until golden brown on the bottom, about 60 seconds. Turn the doughnuts over and fry until the other side is golden, 30 to 60 seconds. Remove with a slotted spoon to paper towels to drain. Dip the tops of the warm doughnuts into the glaze and serve immediately.

MAKES ABOUT 3 CUPS

- 2½ cups confectioners' sugar
- 6 tablespoons fresh apple cider
- ½ teaspoon ground cinnamon (see Note)
- ⅛ teaspoon kosher salt

GLAZE

In a medium bowl, whisk together all of the ingredients.

NOTE: Instead of cinnamon, try any fall spice, such as ginger, nutmeg, or allspice—or a combination.

CHOCOLATE PUDDING

Making chocolate pudding from scratch is rewarding—the difference from store-bought, in flavor and texture, speaks for itself. Indian pudding is a classic New England dish made with cornmeal custard, but personally I find chocolate to be a more decadent treat. This version can be made a day or two in advance. When serving, top with freshly whipped cream.

In a large saucepan, bring the milk, half-and-half, and salt to a boil. Remove from the heat and add the chocolate. Return to medium heat and whisk until the chocolate is completely melted.

In a large bowl, whisk together the egg yolks, cornstarch, vanilla, and granulated sugar. Pour the still-warm chocolate mixture into the egg yolk mixture ¼ cup at a time, whisking thoroughly after each addition. After about 1 cup has been added, the chocolate mixture may be added more quickly. Stir to combine; pour the mixture back into the saucepan and return to medium heat. Cook, whisking constantly, until the mixture begins to thicken, about 5 minutes. As soon as it starts to thicken, whisk for another 15 seconds then remove from the heat and pour into individual serving glasses, about ½ cup per serving. Cover loosely with plastic wrap and refrigerate for 4 hours or overnight.

Preheat the oven to 350°F.

Make the whipped cream: In the bowl of a stand mixer fitted with the whisk attachment, or by hand, whip the cream together with the vanilla and confectioners' sugar until soft peaks form.

Place the walnuts on a baking sheet. Toast in the oven for 8 minutes. Chop the walnuts into small pieces. Serve the pudding topped with whipped cream and the walnuts.

SERVES 6 TO 8

- 2 cups whole milk
- 1 cup half-and-half
- ½ teaspoon kosher salt
- 6 ounces semisweet chocolate, finely chopped (about 1 cup), or semisweet chips
- 3 large egg yolks
- 1 tablespoon cornstarch
- 2 teaspoons plus 2 tablespoons pure vanilla extract
- 6 tablespoons granulated sugar
- 2 cups heavy cream
- 2 tablespoons confectioners' sugar
- ¼ cup walnuts

HOT CHOCOLATE
WITH HOMEMADE MARSHMALLOWS

Homemade marshmallows take effort to prepare, but they are a fun dessert to make with kids, and taste best when served with hot chocolate on a cold winter day. Make hot chocolate in larger batches and warm it up as needed.

MAKES 6 CUPS

FOR THE MARSHMALLOWS

3 ounces unflavored powdered gelatin

1¾ cups granulated sugar

⅔ cup light corn syrup

½ teaspoon kosher salt

1 tablespoon pure vanilla extract

½ cup potato starch

½ cup confectioners' sugar

FOR THE HOT CHOCOLATE

6 cups whole milk

6 ounces bittersweet chocolate, finely grated

½ cup unsweetened cocoa powder

⅔ cup sugar

Make the marshmallows: In the bowl of a stand mixer, sprinkle the gelatin over ½ cup water and let soak for 5 minutes. Fit the mixer with the whisk attachment.

In a small saucepan, combine the granulated sugar, corn syrup, salt, and ½ cup water, then bring to a boil. Lower the heat and simmer until the mixture reaches 240°F on a candy thermometer.

Start whisking the gelatin at low speed. Carefully pour the 240°F sugar mixture into the bowl with the gelatin, increasing the speed as the sugar is added. Whisk until the mixture becomes firm and the volume has increased, about 12 minutes. Whisk in the vanilla, then turn off the mixer.

Coat a 9-inch-square baking dish with nonstick spray. Pour the marshmallow mixture into the baking dish; level the mixture with a spatula. Let sit at room temperature for 5 hours.

Sift the potato starch and confectioners' sugar together into a large bowl. Dust a little of the mixture onto a cutting board. Invert the marshmallow mixture onto the board. Cut the marshmallow into 1-inch squares and toss them gently in the bowl of potato starch and sugar. Store the marshmallows in an airtight container at room temperature for 5 to 7 days.

Make the hot chocolate: In a large saucepan, bring the milk to a boil, then whisk in the chocolate until it is melted. Lower the heat to medium and whisk in the cocoa powder and sugar until everything is dissolved and completely smooth. Pour the hot chocolate into warm mugs and top each serving with 2 marshmallows.

BASICS

PREP TECHNIQUES

CHICKEN STOCK

Chicken stock is a kitchen staple that every cook should master and keep on hand. Stocks should be a base to build flavor. I don't add salt to my stocks, because if you reduce them the salt intensifies.

MAKES ABOUT 1 GALLON

3½ pounds chicken bones and parts, fat trimmed off, rinsed and patted dry

1 large Spanish onion, cut into 2-inch pieces

2 medium carrots, cut into 1-inch pieces

2 stalks celery, cut into 1-inch pieces

1 garlic clove, smashed

4 sprigs fresh thyme

2 bay leaves

10 whole black peppercorns

In a large stockpot, combine the chicken bones and 6 quarts cold water. Slowly bring to a simmer, uncovered, over medium heat; skim off any fat or impurities that float to the surface. When the water is simmering steadily, but not boiling, add the remaining ingredients and simmer for about 4 hours, continuing to skim off any fat or impurities that float to the top as the stock cooks for the first hour.

Strain through a fine-mesh sieve and let cool. Chill the stock completely. Store in an airtight container in the refrigerator for up to 4 days or freeze for up to 1 month.

VARIATION

DARK CHICKEN STOCK: Begin making the stock by roasting the bones in a large roasting pan in the oven at 375°F for 45 minutes. Continue as directed above.

LOBSTER STOCK

Lobster stock is a staple in my kitchen and has many applications. Try cooking grains and legumes in this stock for a flavorful dish. Make a batch when you're using a recipe that calls for only lobster tails and claws and the bodies are leftover. You can freeze the stock in small amounts and only defrost what is needed.

MAKES ABOUT 1 GALLON
---

15 (1½- to 2-pound) lobster bodies

½ cup canola or grape-seed oil

2 cups chopped onion

1 cup chopped fennel bulb

1 cup chopped celery

1 cup chopped carrot

3 cups chopped tomatoes (fresh or canned)

1 (750-ml) bottle white wine

6 sprigs fresh thyme

1 head garlic

6 whole black peppercorns

2 bay leaves

1 cup tomato paste

Split the lobster bodies lengthwise with a cleaver and remove the innards. All dark green roe (and any meat) should be saved for another use. Rinse the shells under cold water and cut them into smaller pieces.

In a large, wide stockpot, heat the oil until it's lightly smoking. Add the lobster shells and stir frequently, letting them cook for 4 to 5 minutes (do not let them burn). Add the onion, fennel, celery, and carrot and continue to cook for 6 to 8 minutes, until the vegetables begin to caramelize. Stir in the tomatoes and wine. Bring to a boil, then add the remaining ingredients and 5 quarts cold water.

RECIPE CONTINUES

Bring back to a light boil and skim off any fat or impurities that float to the top. Reduce to a simmer and cook for about 2½ hours.

Strain through a fine-mesh sieve, making sure to press out all the liquid from the shells. Chill the stock completely. Store in an airtight container in the refrigerator for 2 to 3 days or freeze for up to 1 month.

VEAL STOCK

A good butcher will have veal bones available. Make sure you request that they be split into pieces. The bones will likely come frozen; if so, it's not necessary to thaw them before roasting.

MAKES ABOUT 1 GALLON	
6 pounds veal bones, cut into 3- to 4-inch pieces	¼ cup tomato paste
	1 cup red wine
¼ cup canola oil	2 garlic cloves, smashed
1 carrot, cut into 1-inch pieces	2 bay leaves
1 large onion, cut into 2-inch pieces	2 sprigs fresh thyme
	5 whole black peppercorns
1 stalk celery, cut into 1-inch pieces	

Preheat the oven to 400°F.

In a large roasting pan, roast the veal bones until they've turned a deep brown color, about 1 hour.

In a large stockpot, heat the oil over medium-high heat and add the carrot. Cook, uncovered, until it begins to caramelize, 6 to 7 minutes. Add the onion and cook until it begins to color lightly, another 3 to 4 minutes.

Drain off any excess fat and stir in the celery and tomato paste; cook for 60 seconds, stirring frequently and scraping the bottom of the pan so the tomato paste does not burn. Carefully add the wine and bring to a boil; add the veal bones and remaining ingredients with 2 gallons cold water. Slowly bring back to a simmer; skim off any fat or impurities that float to the top. Let simmer very gently for about 12 hours.

Strain through a fine-mesh sieve. Chill the stock completely. Store in an airtight container in the refrigerator for up to 4 days or freeze for up to 1 month.

VEGETABLE STOCK

Vegetable stock is easy to make; use it for cooking soups and vegetable dishes.

MAKES ABOUT 1 GALLON	
1 small onion, cut into 1-inch pieces	1 small orange wedge
1 carrot, cut into 1-inch pieces	3 cremini mushrooms, chopped
1 stalk celery, cut into 1-inch pieces	2 sprigs fresh thyme
½ Granny Smith apple, cored	3 pieces fresh parsley stem
½ cup chopped fennel bulb	2 bay leaves
	5 whole black peppercorns

In a large stockpot, combine all the ingredients with 5 quarts cold water and bring to a simmer over medium-high heat; cook, uncovered, for 30 minutes.

Let cool for 30 minutes; strain through a fine-mesh sieve. Store in an airtight container in the refrigerator for up to 5 days or freeze for up to 1 month.

MUSHROOM STOCK

Mushrooms create an earthy, delicate broth; I use this stock when cooking vegetable dishes to give them a bit more depth.

MAKES ABOUT 2 QUARTS

3 tablespoons canola oil	12 ounces cremini mushrooms, sliced
2 garlic cloves, smashed	2 sprigs fresh rosemary
2 large shallots, sliced	2 bay leaves
1 leek, split and rinsed	

In a large saucepan, heat the oil over medium-high heat; add the garlic, shallots, and leek. Sweat the vegetables, uncovered, for 1 minute, then add the mushrooms and continue cooking for another 2 minutes. Add the remaining ingredients with 10 cups cold water and bring to a boil; lower the heat to a simmer and cook for 30 minutes.

Let cool for 30 minutes; strain through a fine-mesh sieve. Store in an airtight container in the refrigerator for up to 5 days or freeze for up to 1 month.

BRINE

I like this basic brine for leaner meats such as pork and poultry. It can add great moisture and flavor to the finished product. (I don't usually brine beef, as it has a higher fat content. I turn to rubs and marinades for fattier cuts of meat.) This brine recipe can easily be halved or doubled, depending on the size of the cut of meat you are brining.

To use the brine, submerge the meat in the brine and let sit for 2 to 4 hours. (If longer than 2 hours, place container in the refrigerator.) Remove the meat and air-dry the meat or poultry on a plate for several hours in the refrigerator before cooking.

MAKES ABOUT 1 GALLON

½ cup sugar	1 tablespoon mustard seeds
1 cup kosher salt	1 tablespoon chile flakes
2 garlic cloves	1 small Spanish onion, cut in half
1 sprig fresh thyme	10 cups ice
1 sprig fresh rosemary	

In a large stockpot, combine all of the ingredients except for the ice, add 2 cups water, and bring to a boil.

Put the ice in a container that is large enough to hold the poultry or pork; once the brine has come to a boil, pour it over the ice. (The ice will cool down the brine quickly and dilute it.)

HOMEMADE MAYONNAISE

Making mayonnaise at home is so much more rewarding than buying it. With this recipe, you can really taste the lemon and Dijon. It is a wonderful accompaniment to seafood dishes.

1 large egg yolk

1 tablespoon freshly squeezed lemon juice

1 teaspoon Dijon mustard

½ teaspoon kosher salt

1 cup canola oil

In the bowl of a food processor, combine the egg yolk, lemon juice, mustard, and salt. On the lowest setting, process for 30 seconds, or until smooth. With the processor still running, slowly add the oil in a steady stream. The ingredients should be thoroughly blended, and look thick and glossy. If the mayonnaise gets too thick before all of the oil has been added, drizzle in 1 teaspoon of water at a time to thin.

Store in an airtight container in the refrigerator until ready to use, or for up to 2 days.

AÏOLI

I use aïoli more often than mayonnaise because of its versatility. It is a version of garlic mayonnaise that originated in Provence—I find that the addition of garlic makes it a flavorful dipping sauce and that it can be varied in any number of ways.

2 large egg yolks

2 tablespoons freshly squeezed lemon juice

¼ cup white wine

1 tablespoon Dijon mustard

¼ teaspoon ground cayenne

1 garlic clove

1 cup canola oil

½ cup extra-virgin olive oil

In the bowl of a food processor, combine the egg yolks, lemon juice, wine, mustard, cayenne, and garlic. On the lowest setting, process for 30 seconds, or until smooth. With the processor still running, slowly drizzle in the canola oil and then the olive oil, adding water as needed to thin out the mixture. The aïoli should be shiny and have the consistency of a thin mayonnaise.

Store in an airtight container in the refrigerator until ready to use, or for up to 2 days.

VARIATIONS

HERB: Stir in 2 tablespoons chopped fresh herbs such as tarragon, basil, or oregano to the finished aïoli.

BLACK PEPPER: In a small saucepan, simmer the wine with 1 tablespoon freshly ground black pepper for about 1 minute. Cool completely and continue as directed above.

SMOKED PAPRIKA: In a small saucepan, simmer the wine with 1 tablespoon smoked paprika for about 1 minute. Cool completely and continue as directed above.

SRIRACHA: Add 1 to 4 tablespoons Sriracha or your favorite hot sauce to the aïoli.

COCKTAIL SAUCE

This basic recipe is easy to whip together in time for any seafood feast.

½ cup ketchup

½ cup chili sauce

2 tablespoons prepared horseradish

1 tablespoon red Tabasco sauce

2 teaspoons Worcestershire sauce

1 teaspoon freshly ground black pepper

1 teaspoon kosher salt

In a small bowl, combine all of the ingredients. Serve immediately or transfer to an airtight container and refrigerate for up to 2 weeks.

TARTAR SAUCE

The creamy aïoli combined with the salt from both the pickles and capers in this tartar sauce complements most fried seafood.

1 cup Herb Aïoli (page 222) or Homemade Mayonnaise (page 222)

3 tablespoons minced dill pickles

3 tablespoons minced red onion

1 tablespoon chopped fresh flat-leaf parsley

1 tablespoon freshly squeezed lemon juice

1 tablespoon capers, rinsed and chopped

Kosher salt and freshly ground black pepper

In a medium bowl, combine all of the ingredients. Cover with plastic wrap and refrigerate for at least 1 hour or up to 3 days.

BOILED POTATOES IN VEGETABLE STOCK

I boil potatoes in vegetable stock to deepen their flavor. In order to achieve the right consistency, do not overcook them in the stock. The potatoes should be just tender so that they finish cooking when you brown them in butter. Use the leftover stock to cook rice or other grains, or as the base for a soup.

18 butterball or All-Blue potatoes (the size of a golf ball), skins on and scrubbed

3 quarts Vegetable Stock (page 220)

2 sprigs fresh thyme

1 sprig fresh rosemary

1 garlic clove

1 strip lemon peel

2 tablespoons kosher salt, plus more for seasoning

¼ cup unsalted butter

Freshly ground black pepper

Put the potatoes in a large stockpot with the stock, thyme, rosemary, garlic, lemon peel, and 2 tablespoons salt. (Make sure all of the ingredients are cold.) Cook over medium heat until the ingredients come to a simmer. Reduce the heat so they continue to simmer gently; the potatoes should never boil. Cook for about 20 minutes, or until the potatoes are just tender all the way through (use a thin skewer to check doneness).

RECIPE CONTINUES

Remove from the heat and let the potatoes cool slightly in the cooking liquid, then with a slotted spoon, take them out and cut them in half. (Reserve the stock for another use.)

In a large sauté pan, melt the butter over medium heat. Add the potatoes cut side down and cook until they just begin to brown. Drain off any excess butter; season with salt and pepper before serving.

CRISP FINGERLING POTATOES

Fingerling potatoes cook quickly and easily, making this side a simple addition to a meal.

SERVES 4	
2 sprigs fresh thyme	4 tablespoons unsalted butter
2 pounds thumb-size fingerling potatoes, skin on	Kosher salt and freshly ground black pepper

Preheat the oven to 350°F.

Remove the leaves from the thyme and discard the stems. (You should have about 1 tablespoon thyme.) Rinse the potatoes and cut them in half lengthwise.

In a small saucepan, melt the butter with the thyme leaves over medium heat. Toss the butter with the potatoes and season generously with salt and pepper.

Place the potatoes in a single layer, cut side down, on a baking sheet. Roast for 15 to 20 minutes, until tender. The cut side should be golden brown and crisp.

WARM POTATO SALAD

In my opinion potato salad should be served warm, and that it is best when kept simple. Make sure you use fresh potatoes, preferably purchased at the farmers' market, because the final flavor of the salad depends so much on the quality of the main ingredient.

SERVES 6 TO 8	
1 pound small red potatoes, cut into quarters	1 tablespoon grainy mustard
Kosher salt	3 tablespoons crème fraîche
1 tablespoon sherry vinegar	Freshly ground black pepper

Preheat the oven to 350°F.

In a large stockpot, cover the potatoes with cold water and season with salt. Bring to a boil, then lower the heat to a simmer; cook until the potatoes are tender but not falling apart, about 12 minutes. Drain and spread on a baking sheet. Dry the potatoes in the oven for 4 minutes.

Transfer the potatoes to a large bowl and stir in the vinegar and mustard. Let cool for a few minutes, then stir in the crème fraîche. Season with salt and pepper and keep warm until ready to serve.

VARIATION

This salad can also be served cold. Prepare as directed, then put in an airtight container and chill thoroughly in the refrigerator before serving.

CREAMY WHIPPED POTATOES

One of the tricks I use when cooking these potatoes is to dry them out in the oven after they've been boiled but before they are whipped. This helps lower the moisture content and ultimately results in fluffier potatoes.

SERVES 4	
2 cups heavy cream	Kosher salt and freshly ground black pepper
¾ cup (1½ sticks) unsalted butter	
4 russet potatoes, peeled and cut into 1-inch pieces, placed in a bowl of cold water	

Preheat the oven to 350°F.

In a medium saucepan, heat the cream with the butter over medium heat until the butter is just melted. Remove from the heat and set aside.

Drain the potatoes and put them in a large stockpot; cover with fresh, cold, generously salted water. Bring to a simmer and cook until the potatoes can be easily pierced with a paring knife but are not falling apart, about 12 minutes.

Drain the potatoes and spread them on a baking sheet; dry in the oven for 5 minutes.

Put the potatoes in the bowl of a stand mixer fitted with the whisk attachment. Very slowly, mix the potatoes, adding the cream-butter mixture a little at a time. When all of the liquid has been added, increase the speed to high and whip for 20 seconds, until the potatoes are creamy and light. Season the whipped potatoes with salt and pepper. Place the whipped potatoes in a serving bowl and cover with foil. Keep warm until ready to serve.

VARIATION
SCALLION WHIPPED POTATOES:

After seasoning the whipped potatoes, add 4 thinly sliced scallions (reserve a few slices for garnish); mix thoroughly to incorporate.

HAND-CUT FRIES

Fries are easy to prepare, and the best ones are made at home. Boiling and then freezing the potatoes before frying helps to create perfectly cooked, crisp fries.

SERVES 4	
3 russet potatoes, peeled	3 cups canola oil
¼ cup kosher salt, plus more for seasoning	

Cut the ends off of the potatoes and square off the sides; cut into 1-inch slices, then into ½-inch strips. Put the potato slices in a bowl of cold water until ready to use.

Bring 2 quarts water to a boil with the ¼ cup salt. Drain the potatoes and add them to the boiling water; boil for 1½ minutes. Carefully remove the potatoes from the heat and drain well. Pat dry with a paper towel; place them in an airtight container and freeze for 1 hour, or until ready to use.

RECIPE CONTINUES

In a large, heavy-bottom pan, heat the oil over medium-high heat to 400°F on a deep-frying thermometer. Remove the fries from the freezer and carefully add them to the oil in batches. Cook until golden brown, about 7 minutes. Adjust the heat so the oil stays around 350°F. When the fries are cooked, remove them with a slotted spoon and drain on a paper towel. Season immediately with salt and serve warm.

POTATO CHIPS

Frying a variety of vegetable chips—potato, of course, but also carrot, parsnip, taro root, celery root, sweet potato, or beets—at home is not difficult. It takes a little preparation and patience but can dramatically alter a dish. The trick is to peel and slice the vegetables very thinly and evenly. See the variations below for even more options.

SERVES 4	
1 large russet potato	Kosher salt for seasoning
4 cups canola oil	

Slice the potato very thin using a mandolin or large vegetable peeler. Rinse in cold water and drain well; pat dry with a paper towel.

In a large saucepot, heat the oil to 280°F. Add the potato slices to the oil, a few at a time. (Too many slices at once will cool the oil too quickly; add just enough to cover the surface area of the oil.) Fry slowly, stirring the slices occasionally to ensure they cook evenly. The frying time will vary depending on the thickness, but the chips should become golden brown around the edges and start to hold a shape after 2 to 3 minutes.

Transfer the chips to a paper towel and season with salt. The chips and all the variations can be made up to 2 days in advance. Store in an airtight container at room temperature.

VARIATIONS

SUNCHOKE CRISPS: Slice a 3-inch piece of sunchoke and fry in ¾ cup canola oil at 300°F.

CRISP SHALLOTS: Slice 1 large shallot into thin rounds. Season ¼ cup flour liberally with kosher salt and freshly ground black pepper. Dredge the shallot rounds in the flour. Heat 1 cup canola oil over high heat. Fry the shallots quickly, for about 20 seconds or until just starting to crisp.

ARTICHOKE CHIPS: With a paring knife, remove all of the dark green artichoke leaves. When you reach the pale yellow heart, scoop out the prickly center of the choke. With a mandolin or very sharp knife, shave the artichoke heart. In a heavy-bottom pot, heat oil to 300°F. Crisp quickly in the oil, about 30 to 45 seconds for each.

FRIED GARLIC TOPS: Wash and pat dry the green tops of 5 stalks of green garlic. With a sharp knife, slice the tops at an angle into thin strips; they should be in a V-shape after they're cut. In a heavy-bottom sauté pan, heat 3 cups canola oil to 275°F. Fry the garlic strips until they begin to color very lightly around the edges, about 2 minutes. (They should still have a deep green color after frying.)

ROASTED PUMPKIN SEEDS

Seeds from 1 pumpkin (about 1 cup)	1 teaspoon kosher salt
2 tablespoons unsalted butter	

Preheat the oven to 350°F.

Wash the pumpkin seeds and pat dry.

In a small saucepan, melt the butter. Add the seeds and toss to coat.

Spread the seeds on a baking sheet and roast until golden brown, about 7 to 9 minutes. Season with salt.

PLAIN PASTA DOUGH

Making homemade pasta dough takes practice but is a simple task that results in greater texture and flavor than dried pasta.

MAKES ABOUT 1 POUND, OR 6 TO 8 SERVINGS

2 cups all-purpose flour, plus extra for dusting	5 large egg yolks
	1 large whole egg
Pinch of kosher salt	2 tablespoons extra-virgin olive oil

In a large bowl, combine the flour and salt. Make a well in the middle of the flour.

In a separate medium bowl, combine the egg yolks, whole egg, oil, and ¼ cup water. Pour the egg mixture into the well of the flour and begin to slowly incorporate the flour mixture into the egg with a rubber spatula until it starts to form into a ball. (For this small amount of dough, I find it easier to mix by hand. Alternatively, combine in a stand mixer fitted with the dough hook, on a medium setting. The dough will come together much more quickly, and will only take 4 to 5 minutes total in the stand mixer.)

To knead and roll out dough: Transfer the dough to a floured surface and knead until it is well mixed and has a firm, smooth feel, 5 to 6 minutes. Wrap the dough loosely in plastic wrap and refrigerate for 1 hour before rolling out. (The dough can be refrigerated for up to 24 hours before using.)

Cut the dough into four equal pieces. Roll one piece into a rectangle that is thin enough to be fed through a manual pasta-

RECIPE CONTINUES

RECIPE CONTINUED

rolling machine. Put the dough through the roller starting at the highest setting and work your way down until the pasta is at the desired thickness. Repeat with the remaining pieces. (If you are rolling by hand, roll the dough to the desired thinness, allowing it to rest, covered, for 10 minutes if it becomes too difficult to roll out.) If necessary, dust the dough with extra flour to make sure that it does not stick to itself, the machine, or the work surface. Once rolled out, cut the pasta into a particular shape or fill it as directed in the recipe in which you're using it.

BUCKWHEAT PASTA DOUGH

The buckwheat flour in this recipe makes for a firmer, slightly drier dough than plain pasta. If the consistency is too dry, knead the dough for 2 or 3 minutes, then let it rest for 10 minutes before kneading again.

MAKES ABOUT 1 POUND, OR 6 TO 8 SERVINGS

¾ cup buckwheat flour

¼ cup all-purpose flour, plus a little extra for dusting

Pinch of kosher salt

2 large egg yolks

1 large whole egg

1 tablespoon extra-virgin olive oil

In a large bowl, combine both flours and the salt. Make a well in the middle of the flour.

In a separate bowl, combine the egg yolks, whole egg, oil, and 2 tablespoons water. Pour the egg mixture into the well of the flour and begin to slowly incorporate the flour mixture into the egg with a rubber spatula until it starts to form into a ball. (For this small amount of dough, I find it easier to mix by hand. Alternatively, combine in a stand mixer fitted with the dough hook, on a medium setting. The dough will come together much more quickly, and will only take 4 to 5 minutes total in the stand mixer.)

For directions on how to knead and roll out the pasta, see page 228.

PASTRY DOUGH

This is a fairly basic, versatile dough that can be used to make pies or tarts. The trick is to not overwork the dough, and to let it rest and chill before rolling it out.

MAKES ¼ POUND

1½ cups all-purpose flour, plus more for dusting

¼ teaspoon kosher salt

¾ cup (1½ sticks) cold unsalted butter, cut into ¼-inch pieces

¼ cup plus 1 tablespoon ice water

In a food processor, combine the flour and salt and pulse to mix. Add the butter; pulse until it is the size of small peas. Sprinkle in the ice water and pulse just until the pastry starts to come together. (If mixing by hand, combine in a large bowl and cut in butter with a pastry cutter or two butter knives. Mix in the ice water using a rubber spatula.)

Turn the dough out onto a lightly floured surface and pat it into a disk shape. The dough may be a little dry, but will hydrate as it rests.

Wrap the dough in plastic wrap and refrigerate for 2 hours, or until firm.

RUSTIC BREAD

New England settlers once made hearty rustic breads. My version results in a crisp crust with an airy interior and can be used to accompany a variety of dishes.

MAKES 2 (1½-POUND) LOAVES	
1 pound, 9 ounces bread flour	3 ounces whole wheat flour
1 pound, 3 ounces water	¾ ounce kosher salt (about 1 tablespoon)
½ teaspoon active dry yeast	Oil for the bowl

Make the sourdough starter: In a large, glass bowl, combine 4 ounces bread flour, 5 ounces water, and ½ teaspoon yeast. Let sit at room temperature (around 72°F) for 12 to 16 hours. The mixture should double in size and then deflate, and have a slightly sour smell to it.

Make the dough: When the starter is ready, pour the remaining 14 ounces water into the bowl of a stand mixer fitted with the paddle attachment, or into a large mixing bowl. Add the sourdough starter, the remaining 1 pound, 5 ounces bread flour, the whole wheat flour, and salt. Mix on low speed for 6 minutes, or mix with a spatula until the mixture forms into a ball.

Transfer the dough to a lightly floured surface. Knead by hand for 8 to 10 minutes. Place the dough in a lightly greased large bowl and cover loosely with a kitchen towel or plastic wrap.

Let stand at room temperature for about 1 hour 15 minutes. Punch down the dough,

then let rise for another 1 hour 15 minutes. The dough should be about double its original size. (If it takes longer, don't panic. Due to the small amount of yeast, it will be slower to rise but will result in a richer flavor.)

On a lightly floured surface, divide the dough in half and **[1]** shape loosely into

rounds. Let sit for 5 minutes. **[2]** With floured hands, pat the dough out into a circle, then roll out and pat the dough into a log shape, making the middle thicker than the ends. **[3]** Tuck the ends under to create a fairly even-shaped loaf. Repeat with the other half.

Place the loaves on a well-floured surface, cover with a kitchen towel, and let stand at room temperature for 1½ to 2 hours.

Preheat the oven to 450°F.

If you have a pizza stone, place the stone in the oven while preheating. If not, use an upside-down baking sheet. Fill a medium saucepot with 4 to 5 cups water; place it on the floor of your oven to create steam. This will help to form a nice crust on the bread.

When the oven and stone (or baking sheet) are preheated, **[4]** use a sharp knife or razor to lightly slash the top of each loaf down the center; if your loaves are about 12 inches long, the slash should be about 8 inches long and ¼ inch deep. Carefully slide the loaves onto the heated baking stone or pan. When the loaves are in the oven, make sure the oven door remains closed to help keep the steam in and bake for 20 to 25 minutes, or until the crust is a deep golden brown. Transfer the loaves to a wire rack and let cool completely. The bread can be made 2 days in advance; once cool, wrap tightly in plastic wrap and store at room temperature.

U.S. AND METRIC CONVERSION CHARTS
All conversions are approximate.

WEIGHT CONVERSIONS

U.S./U.K.	Metric
½ oz	14 g
1 oz	28 g
1½ oz	43 g
2 oz	57 g
2½ oz	71 g
3 oz	85 g
3½ oz	100 g
4 oz	113 g
5 oz	142 g
6 oz	170 g
7 oz	200 g
8 oz	227 g
9 oz	255 g
10 oz	284 g
11 oz	312 g
12 oz	340 g
13 oz	368 g
14 oz	400 g
15 oz	425 g
1 lb	454 g

OVEN TEMPERATURES

°F	Gas Mark	°C
250	½	120
275	1	140
300	2	150
325	3	165
350	4	180
375	5	190
400	6	200
425	7	220
450	8	230
475	9	240
500	10	260
550	Broil	290

LIQUID CONVERSIONS

U.S.	Metric
1 tsp	5 ml
1 tbs	15 ml
2 tbs	30 ml
3 tbs	45 ml
¼ cup	60 ml
⅓ cup	75 ml
⅓ cup + 1 tbs	90 ml
⅓ cup + 2 tbs	100 ml
½ cup	120 ml
⅔ cup	150 ml
¾ cup	180 ml
¾ cup + 2 tbs	200 ml
1 cup	240 ml

U.S.	Metric
1 cup	240 ml
1 cup + 2 tbs	275 ml
1¼ cups	300 ml
1⅓ cups	325 ml
1½ cups	350 ml
1⅔ cups	375 ml
1¾ cups	400 ml
1¾ cups + 2 tbs	450 ml
2 cups (1 pint)	475 ml
2½ cups	600 ml
3 cups	720 ml
4 cups (1 quart)	945 ml
	(1,000 ml=1 liter)

HOW TO SHUCK AN OYSTER

The best way to perfect the technique is with practice. Oysters have a top and a bottom; the flatter shell is the top and the rounded one is the bottom. The hinge that connects the two shells is the best point of entry when shucking.

1. Place the oyster on top of a clean towel with the bottom (round) shell down against a firm surface. Wrap the towel around the rounded edge of the oyster so that the hinge is exposed.

2. Hold the towel-wrapped oyster firmly in place with one hand—the towel will protect your hand. Use your other hand to place the tip of an oyster knife into the hinge, between the two shells.

3. Push the knife into the hinge, twisting back and forth with firm pressure until the tip of the knife is planted firmly between the shells. (You should be able to hold up the knife without losing the oyster.)

4. Turn the knife 90 degrees, twisting the blade until you feel the top shell "pop" off the lower shell.

5. Keeping the oyster level (so that you don't lose any liquid), slide the knife along the

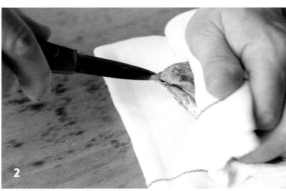

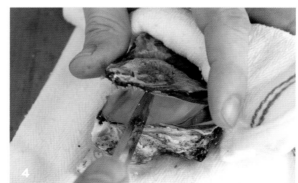

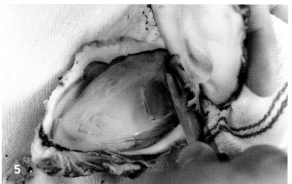

inside of the top shell to loosen the oyster meat from the shell. Remove the top shell completely. Carefully slide the knife under the oyster meat against the bottom shell to loosen the connective muscle from the shell. **6.** Place on ice and serve at once.

HOW TO FILLET A FLATFISH

Flatfish have both eyes on one side of their head. Such fish, like flounder and halibut, are usually delicate and fairly easy to fillet. Use a thin filleting knife that has a little flexibility to the blade. When filleting, make steady, smooth strokes as you cut. The blade should be touching bone on almost every cut: That will give you a reference point so that you know where the blade is even when you can't see what you're cutting. Most smaller flatfish, like flounder, are sold intact, so you have to first remove the innards.

1. Pat the fish dry with a paper towel and place on a dry cutting board. Position the fish so that the white side is down and the head is angled away from you. You will notice on one side of the fish, just next to the head, there is a soft pocket; this contains the innards.

2. Starting just below the eyes, make a diagonal cut across the fish just under the pectoral fin—the line should start at the top of the fish and come to a point just below the innards at the bottom of the fish. If you accidentally cut into the guts, make a new cut below that point.

3. You will notice a line that runs down the center of the fish; this line is positioned above the fish's backbone. Following that line, slice the fish from the head to the tail (ignore the curve the line makes at the head). The blade should run along the backbone of the fish—don't apply too much pressure or you'll cut through the delicate bones.

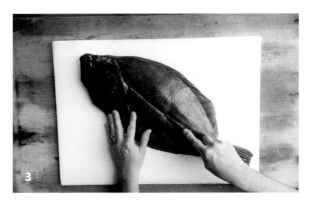

4. Starting at the tail end, place the blade of the knife into the incision you made against the backbone. Keep the blade flat (horizontal) but angled down slightly so that it lays against the bones; working on the side of the fish closest to you, smoothly cut the flesh away from the bone, moving closer to the head with each slice (use your other hand to pull the flesh back as you cut.) For the top fillet, start by inserting your knife in between the flesh and the bones near the head of the fish. Using long strokes, slice the top fillet from the bone just as you did with the bottom fillet (blade angled down, holding the flesh with your other hand.)

5. Turn the fish over and repeat the process, starting with the incisions. Use long strokes and keep the blade flat as you remove the bottom fillet, then the top fillet.

6. To remove the skin, lay the fillets flat, skin side down, on the cutting board with the tail end closest to you. Make a small cut between the skin and the flesh at the tail end. Keep your blade between the skin and flesh; hold the skin firmly with one hand and gently pull it towards you as you push the knife away from you. Using a gentle side-to-side motion with the hand that's holding the skin, slice the flesh away (this will make it easier to move the knife). Be careful not to cut through the skin; slide the blade all the way down to the other end of the fillet. Trim any loose pieces away from the fillet and keep chilled until ready to use.

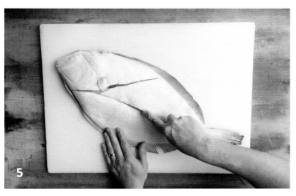

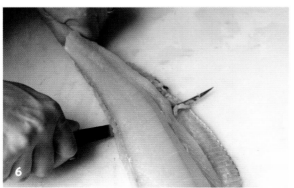

HOW TO FILLET A ROUND FISH

There are many types of round fish, and many have different bone structures and need to be filleted differently. Following is the technique I use when filleting arctic char, small bass, trout, salmon, and bluefish. I would leave larger fish to a trusted fishmonger (it would be a challenge to get a 15-pound striped bass into your refrigerator at home anyway). The best tool for filleting fish is a sharp, thin blade that has a little flexibility.

1. Pat the fish dry with a paper towel and place it flat on a dry cutting board with the head facing to the right and the belly away from you.

2. Just below the gill opening on the head, cut into the fish until you feel the knife hit the backbone (be careful not to cut through the bone). Cut all the way through the belly side to a point just below the pectoral fin.

3. Using the first incision as a guide, place the heel of your knife into the cut so that it is resting on the backbone. Place your other hand firmly on top of the fish (do not push down). Now, turn the knife so that the blade is laying flat against the backbone.

4. Holding the top of the fish, slice the blade across the fish towards the tail. The blade should be angled downward slightly, and you should hear and feel the knife cutting through small bones, but not through the backbone **(A)**. Make sure the blade of the knife is slicing all of the flesh, from belly to backbone. Cut all the way down to the tail; the fillet should come off the fish easily **(B)**.

5. Turn the fish over so the belly is facing you and repeat the process, starting with the first cut just below the gill opening.

6. To remove the belly bones, turn the fillets over so they are skin side down. Use the tip of your knife to loosen the bones from the flesh. With the blade angled up slightly, slice directly under the bones to remove them from the flesh. When you reach the belly of the fillet, towards the end of the bones, turn the blade so that it makes a 90-degree angle and cut through the skin to fully remove the bones.

DIRECTIONS CONTINUE

DIRECTIONS CONTINUED

7. To remove the skin, lay the fillet flat, skin side down, on the cutting board with the tail end angled toward you. Make a small cut between the flesh and the skin at the tail end. If the fish is large enough, pierce the skin at this end to create a small hole—this will help you hold on to the skin. Keep the blade between the flesh and the skin and pull the tail up slightly. The blade should be angled toward the cutting board; pull the skin toward you while pushing the knife away. Making a slight side-to-side motion with the skin will help work the knife through the fillet.

8. To remove the pin bones, use a pair of pliers or fish tweezers. Pull out each bone in the direction that it might have gone in. Be careful when pulling so you don't create gaps in the fillet. Use firm, consistent pressure; try not to tug too hard or to rip them out.

9. Cut the filleted fish into individual portions, about 4 to 6 ounces per serving.

8

7

9

HOW TO STEAM & EAT A LOBSTER

SERVES 6

2 lemons, each cut into 4 pieces

1 fennel bulb, cut into 1-inch pieces

3 stalks celery, chopped

1 large Spanish onion, cut into 1-inch pieces

4 sprigs fresh thyme

2 large bay leaves

6 (1¼- to 1½-pound) lobsters

1. In a pan that's large enough to hold all of the lobsters without piling them on top of one another, place the lemons, fennel, celery, onion, thyme, and bay leaves. Place the lobsters on top of the vegetables and pour about 1 quart water into the pan. The water should come up to the bottom edge of the lobsters.

2. Cover and bring to a simmer over medium-high heat. Once the water starts steaming, reduce the heat and cook for 14 minutes. The water should not be boiling; keep it at a low simmer.

3. If cooking for later use, remove the lobsters and plunge into ice water; let cool for 15 minutes. Remove from ice water and store in the refrigerator.

DIRECTIONS CONTINUE

HOW TO EAT A STEAMED LOBSTER

Once the lobster is steamed, follow my efficient method to get the meat out instead of using an old-fashioned pair of lobster crackers. Hold the hot lobster with a kitchen towel. There will be a mess of liquid and lobster parts during the process, so do this near a sink or over a large bowl.

1. Remove the tail and claws from the body by twisting them off slowly to keep from splattering. Discard the body.
2. Separate the knuckles from the claw by holding the claw and pressing the knuckles firmly against a table or counter until they snap off.
3. Use a cocktail fork and pull the meat from the knuckle at either end.

4. Pull the moveable piece of the claw outward until it becomes loose; carefully remove this "thumb" joint from the larger part of the claw. A small piece of cartilage in the claw should come out with the moveable piece. (If it does not come out, you will have to carefully separate it from the meat after you've removed it from the shell.)

5. Hold the claw firmly by the pincher end and place it down on a cutting board so that it stands horizontally. With a heavy knife, crack the shell at the midpoint of the claw without cutting through the shell or meat. Twist the knife to the side to create a larger opening. The shell should break apart at the cut; if it does not, turn the claw over and repeat.

6. Once the base of the shell has come off, exposing the meat, carefully pull the meat from the claw. Repeat with the second claw.

7. Place the tail shell side up on a counter top. Pull the flipper end of the tail upward until it cracks off the tail.

8. Turn the tail on its side and firmly press down with the heel of your hand until the shell starts to crack.

9. Pick up the tail and pull the underside of the shell outward to crack the shell in half and separate the halves; the meat should come out in one whole piece.

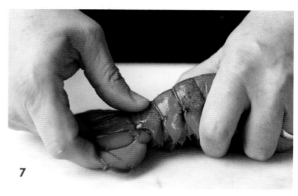

7

8

5

6

9

HOW TO MAKE SLAB BACON

Homemade bacon is an easy and rewarding project to take on at home. The curing and smoking process takes some time, but the sweet, salty results are well worth it.

MAKES ABOUT 2 POUNDS

---

1 cup kosher salt

½ cup sugar

2 tablespoons chopped fresh rosemary

3 garlic cloves, smashed and roughly chopped

1 (2-pound) piece fresh pork belly, skin on

½ cup Vermont Grade A maple syrup

1. In a bowl, combine the salt, sugar, rosemary, and garlic; rub three quarters of this mixture all over the outside of the pork belly. Sprinkle half of the remaining mixture over the bottom of a flat plastic container that is about the same size as the belly. Put the belly in the container and push it firmly into the salt mixture. Sprinkle the remaining mixture over the top of the belly.

2. Drizzle the syrup over the belly and cover the container with plastic wrap.

3. Let the belly cure in the refrigerator for 2 days. Flip the belly over and spoon some of the liquid over the top; continue curing in the refrigerator for another 24 hours.

4. To finish the bacon, heat a charcoal grill with a very small fire and place soaked apple chips on the fire. Put the bacon on the grill and cover. Let

smoke and cook for 40 minutes. There should be a heavy, dark brown smoky layer on the outside of the belly and the meat should register an internal temperature of 150°F.

5. Let cool slightly, then slice away the skin.

6. Cut as directed by a particular recipe (sliced thick or thin or cut into large chunks). Let cool completely; store in an airtight container in the refrigerator for up to 7 days.

5

6

RESOURCES

While most of the ingredients in this cookbook are available at markets, I recommend a number of purveyors from New England and beyond, for sourcing those hard-to-find ingredients. Here are a few of my favorites.

BEER

MAINE BEER COMPANY
525 U.S. Route One
Freeport, Maine 04032
(207) 221-5711
www.mainebeercompany.com

CHEESE

THE CHEESE IRON
200 U.S. Route One, Suite 300
Scarborough, Maine 04074
(207) 883-4057
www.thecheeseiron.com

FARMSTEAD
186 Wayland Avenue
Providence, Rhode Island 02906
(401) 274-7177
www.farmsteadinc.com

FORMAGGIO KITCHEN
244 Huron Avenue
Cambridge, Massachusetts 02138
and
268 Shawmut Avenue
Boston, Massachusetts 02118
(888) 212-3224
www.formaggiokitchen.com

VERMONT BUTTER & CHEESE CREAMERY
www.vermontcreamery.com

MEATS

D'ARTAGNAN
www.dartagnan.com

M. F. DULOCK
201a Highland Avenue
Somerville, Massachusetts 02143
(617) 666-1970
www.mfdulock.com

VERMONT QUALITY MEATS
28 Allen Street
Rutland, Vermont 05701
(802) 747-5950
www.vtqualitymeats.com

PRODUCE

GREENLAW GARDENS
110 Wilson Road
Kittery, Maine 03904
(207) 286-7767
www.facebook.com/GreenlawGardens

PETE'S GREENS
266 South Craftsbury Road
Craftsbury, Vermont 05826
(802) 586-2882
www.petesgreens.com

RUSSO'S
560 Pleasant Street
Watertown, Massachusetts 02472
(617) 923-1500
www.russos.com

WALKER'S ROADSIDE STAND
261 West Main Road
Little Compton, Rhode Island 02837
(401) 635-4719

WARD'S BERRY FARM
614 South Main Street
Sharon, Massachusetts 02067
(781) 784-3600
www.wardsberryfarm.com

SEAFOOD

BOB'S CLAM HUT
315 U.S. 1
Kittery, Maine 03904
(207) 439-4233
www.bobsclamhut.com

CAPTAIN MARDEN'S SEAFOODS
279 Linden Street
Wellesley, Massachusetts 02482
(800) 666-0860
www.captainmardens.com

ISLAND CREEK OYSTERS
296 Parks Street
Duxbury, Massachusetts 02332
(781) 934-2028
www.islandcreekoysters.com

RED'S BEST
13 Fish Pier Street, West
Boston, Massachusetts 02210
(617) 830-1672
www.redsbest.com

SUNNY'S SEAFOOD
Bay One, Boston Fish Pier
Boston, Massachusetts 02210
(617) 261-7123
www.sunnysboston.com

HOME AND KITCHEN

BREVILLE
www.brevilleusa.com

CHINA FAIR
70 Needham Street
Newton, Massachusetts 02461
(617) 332-1250
www.chinafairinc.com

DIDRIK'S
190 Concord Avenue
Cambridge, Massachusetts 02138
(617) 354-5700
www.didriks.com

HEATH CERAMICS
www.heathceramics.com

JB PRINCE
36 East 31st Street
New York, New York 10016
(800) 473-0577
www.jbprince.com

JONO PANDOLFI
www.jonopandolfi.com

KITCHENWARES
215 Newbury Street
Boston, Massachusetts 02116
(857) 366-4237
www.kitchenwaresboston.com

LEKKER
1313 Washington Street
Boston, Massachusetts 02118
(877) 737-7308
www.lekkerhome.com

NEW ENGLAND CHEESES

Here are a few of our favorite New England cheeses listed from mild to pungent. They pair well with Spiced Nuts and Rhubard Compote (see recipes on pages 26 and 27).

BONNE BOUCHE (GOAT'S MILK)
WEBSTERVILLE, VERMONT

Vermont Butter & Cheese is a pioneering operation making fresh and aged goat's milk cheeses. Bonne Bouche is considered their flagship and is a delightful, ash-ripened goat's milk cheese offering a bright flavor balanced with notes of freshly baked bread.

VERANO (SHEEP'S MILK)
WESTMINSTER, VERMONT

Verano is a seasonal cheese, made in the summer when the sheep are feasting on wild herbs and grasses. This summer diet creates a firm sheep's milk cheese with an herbaceous and floral flavor. Verano is made in the early spring through the summer and then aged for three to five months.

BROTHER'S WALK (GOAT'S MILK)
HARDWICK, MASSACHUSETTS

Some cheese lovers argue that you can't find a good brie-style cheese outside of France. Brother's Walk begs to differ. Made at Ruggles Hill Farm, Brother's Walk is a goat's milk brie that combines bright flavors with a cheesemaking process that creates a soft, spreadable cheese. The result is rich and delicious.

CABOT CLOTHBOUND CHEDDAR (COW'S MILK)
GREENSBORO, VERMONT

A partnership between legendary Cabot Cheese and the innovative Cellars at Jasper Hill, this large wheel of cheddar is made by Cabot and hand delivered to the Cellars at Jasper Hill for about ten months of aging. The end product has incredible structure and evokes tropical pineapple with an underlying savory quality.

PRESCOTT (COW'S MILK)
HARDWICK, MASSACHUSETTS

Located just outside of Boston, Robinson Dairy is making firm, washed-rind cheeses that resemble the famed alpine cheeses of Germany and Austria. We recommend Prescott, a dense alpine-style cheese with a nutty flavor.

WINNEMERE (COW'S MILK)
GREENSBORO, VERMONT

This cheese, which is wrapped in spruce bark and then washed with beer, is perfect when you're looking for an excuse to stay in and relax. The spruce and washing process create a woodsy, earthy, and luscious cheese meant to fortify.

ACKNOWLEDGMENTS

Creating *The New England Kitchen* was an intense and lengthy process but well worth the effort, and it would be almost impossible to acknowledge everyone who made the book happen—but I will try. When **Erin Byers Murray** and I first sat down to work on the project, we both had kids on the way: Those babies are now three years old. Erin has been a longtime friend, and I couldn't imagine working on this cookbook with anyone else. She showed patience and grace throughout this project when I needed it most. I have been blessed with an amazing staff that handled so much when I needed them to: **Nicki Hobson, Lauren Kroesser, Francisco Millan, Rich Morin, Amy Audette, Ashley, Max, Kirsten, Aldamar, Tom, Tim, Val,** and **everyone who works so hard every day at Lineage, Island Creek Oyster Bar,** and **Row 34.** Andrew Holden and his Eastern Standard team, including **Molly Hopper Sandrof,** who shares her impressive knowledge of cheese on these pages: Thank you!

A thank-you also goes to **all of the New England chefs** who have come before me and are working so hard now to continue to shape our region's culinary identity and to make this a special place to eat and cook.

I also have to thank the best business partners and friends that a chef could ask for: **Garret Harker, Skip Bennett,** and **Shore Gregory.** You guys make it fun, and I feel so lucky to be collaborating with you. Special thanks to **Paula Harker, cousin Mark, the ICO crew,** and **all the farmers and fishermen who contributed,** some without even knowing it. A big thank-you to **Sandy Gilbert at Rizzoli** for pushing us to make such a beautiful book, and to **Danielle Chiotti** for her enthusiasm and patience. The photographs by **Michael Harlan Turkell** were just a small part of his contribution to this cookbook. His experience, advice, and pizza got me through the demanding days. Thank you to **Molly Shuster** for her teamwork and for helping to make each shot beautiful, and to graphic designer **Amy Sly** for laying the book out in such a thoughtful way.

Carol Glagola, you arrived at the perfect time—honestly, I could not have accomplished this project without you. Thank you for everything that you do.

Thanks to **my sisters, Jennifer, Mary,** and **Amanda,** for being supportive of their brother and for putting up with me longer than most have had to; and, of course, to **Jean Marie** for always being on target. For the people who pushed, inspired, and encouraged me more than anyone else—**my dad, Stan, Gethin Thomas,** and **Corky Clark:** Thank you for shaping me into the person I am today—in and out of the kitchen.

Lisa, Hudson, Ethan, and **Sophia:** Thank you, all, for being the best family anyone could ever have!

—JEREMY SEWALL

My biggest thanks go to **Jeremy Sewall** for creating recipes that make me want to get into the kitchen and cook. I'd also like to thank our agent, **Danielle Chiotti**, at Upstart Crow, for being a constant source of positivity, and our editor, **Sandy Gilbert**, and her research assistant, **Hilary S. Ney**, at Rizzoli; Sandy has been an excellent coach and teacher. And thanks to all of those who tested recipes and offered genuine feed-back, including Dottie and Kelly Byers, Jeannie and Glen Barker, Dottie and Joe Distelheim, Sansing and Terry McPherson, Carol and Jim Williams, and Lynn and Mike Pellegrino.

And, of course, thanks to **my husband, Dave**, and **son, Charlie**, who were patient with me through the long days and who served as critical taste testers along the way.

—ERIN BYERS MURRAY

INDEX

Page numbers in *italics* indicate illustrations